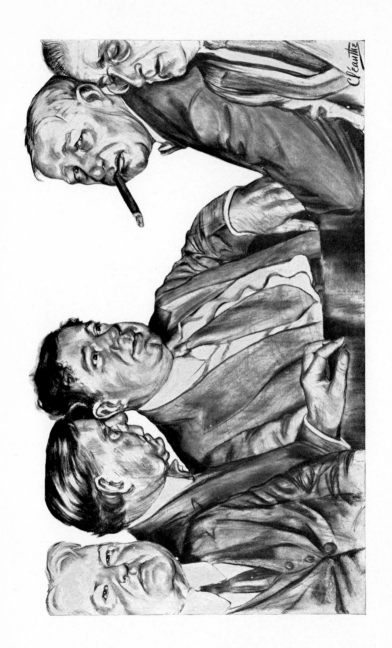

My First Days

in

The White House

by

HUEY PIERCE LONG

❧

Dedicated to
The Lazarus of Today and Tomorrow

❧

The Telegraph Press, Harrisburg, Pa.

1935

PRINTED IN THE UNITED STATES OF AMERICA
BY THE TELEGRAPH PRESS, HARRISBURG, PA

Foreword

THIS *volume is presented as a prophecy by its Author, the late Huey Pierce Long, wherein he endeavored to portray what he would have done had he become President and how he would have conducted national government; setting forth his impressions of what he believed would be the reaction of the people referred to and the public, generally.*

This book has been published in good faith, without malice, but with a desire to present to its readers a future America under the guidance of its Author.

Illustrations by

Cléanthe

New York - Paris

Table of Contents

INVICTUS!

I

Wherein a New President Takes Office and Outlines a Program to Share Our Wealth

The bitter campaign of 1 9 3 6; inauguration and speech of the new President; the selection of a cabinet; laws outlined to survey wealth and poverty; s t a t e s' organizations for problems at hand.

My First Days in the White House

IT HAD happened. The people had endorsed my plan for the redistribution of wealth and I was President of the United States. I had just sworn upon the Bible from which my father read to us as children to uphold the Constitution and to defend my country against all enemies, foreign and domestic.

Yet standing there on the flag-draped platform erected above the East portico of the Capitol, delivering my inaugural address, it all seemed unreal. I felt that I was dreaming. The great campaign which was destined to save America from Communism and Fascism was history. Other politicians had promised to re-make America; I had promised to sustain it.

The campaign had been bitter. I was cartooned and caricatured unmercifully in some of the newspapers. About the most striking example of the venom of my opposition was shown in a cartoon of an evening newspaper published in the City of New York under the title: "Invictus!" which I have had my artist reproduce in this volume.

As my eyes swept the throng before me, I paused in my inaugural address and looked into the face of the retiring president. He seemed worn and tired. He wore the same expression of resigned fatigue that I had observed in the face of President Hoover on Inauguration Day in 1933 when Mr. Roosevelt declared so confidently that: "The only thing we have to fear is fear itself."

And with all humility, fully conscious of the solemnity of the promise I was making, I laid aside my prepared speech and closed my inaugural address extemporaneously with these words:

> I promise life to the guaranties of our immortal document, the Declaration of Independence, which has decreed that all shall be born equal, and by this I mean that children shall not come into this life burdened with debt, but on the contrary, shall inherit the right to life, liberty and such education and training as qualifies them and equips them to take their proper rank in the pursuance of the occupation and vocation wherein they are worth most to themselves and to this country. And now I must be about my work.

The former president arose and seized my hands. He shouted something in my ear but his words were drowned by the roar from the crowd.

I left the platform immediately.   The secret

service men hurried me into an open car. On the twelve-minute ride to the White House we went down historic Pennsylvania Avenue, where hundreds of thousands of people lined the curb. When I reached the White House, into which so many Presidents had entered in confusion and from which they had departed in bewilderment, I sensed anew the tremendous responsibilities I had assumed as President of the United States.

My family and intimate friends soon arrived from the Capitol. We ate lunch, and then went out to the sheltered grandstand on the Avenue in front of the White House to review the inaugural parade. Two hours later, as the parade ended, I went to the executive offices of the White House, and there sought seclusion.

I was alone. The mass of tasks confronting me was bewildering. I was aware that I would have to disengage myself from the detailed functions of administering the government. I decided to delegate authority to hands not only wholly competent, but generally recognized to be honest and courageous as well.

Installed as the Chief Executive of the United States, and officially acting as such, I drafted a message to the Senate of the United States, as follows:

To the Senate of the United States:

I have the honor to nominate, and by and with your consent will appoint the following members of my cabinet, viz:—

For Secretary of State: William E. Borah of Idaho.

For Secretary of the Treasury: James Couzens of Michigan.

For Secretary of War: Smedley D. Butler of Pennsylvania.

For Secretary of the Navy: Franklin D. Roosevelt of New York.

For Secretary of the Interior: Major General Lytle Brown of Tennessee.

For Secretary of Commerce: Herbert Hoover of California.

For Attorney General: Frank Murphy of Michigan.

For Secretary of Labor: Edward Keating of Colorado.

The farmers' organizations throughout the country had for many years been promised an administration of the Department of Agriculture by persons experienced in the farm work and problems. I concluded, at last, to make this promise a reality. Therefore, I announced that my choice for Secretary of Agriculture would be made from the recommendations of the farm organizations.

At a joint meeting these farmers' agencies unanimously selected one of the best friends I had ever had and whose advice had been of paramount importance to me in the platform I had adopted for agriculture.

It had become clear to my mind that the Postal Service was performing so many business functions of the country that it would have to be eliminated from the category of politics and that the management of the several functions of that enterprise should be entrusted to someone thoroughly acquainted with and recognized as competent in the several fields of its service. I therefore announced that the Postmaster General, as well as all other executives handling the affairs of the Post Office Department, would be selected from the list of agents and employees, according to their merit and record of service.

The Postmaster General for my cabinet was selected in that manner and his name was later sent to the Senate. The young man whom I selected to handle the Post Office Department had begun as a letter carrier in a city of a western state. He rose to the position of Postmaster General on merited service at the age of 42.

I called my secretary and dispatched two messages to the Senate, inasmuch as I desired to send a special message to indicate the method by which the Postmaster General and Secretary of Agriculture had been selected. The Senate was to meet in special session at four o'clock for the purpose of receiving my cabinet nominations.

Then, I drew forward another form, used for the appointment of officials directly under the President. On it, I wrote:

The White House, January 20, 1937.
I hereby appoint Alfred E. Smith to be Director of the Budget.
HUEY PIERCE LONG.

All nominations were confirmed by the Senate at four o'clock P. M., without debate.

I then retired to the second floor of the White House proper and went to the window in a study overlooking the Avenue. I could see the marching throngs parading happily up and down that historic street.

"Could other Presidents have had such confident throngs as these?" I asked myself. "Surely, these surging demonstrations are the result of assured expectation—that I will fulfill pledges which I made. The best of my skill must be applied to that task. There shall be no more disappointment to the American people on the question of my fulfilling a promise than there was to the people of Louisiana."

Suddenly a throng entered the White House grounds, headed by a brass band. The throng marched up in front of the main steps and began to serenade.

The celebration that followed was quite orderly. I saw two youths suddenly unroll a banner. On it were the words:

"ON OUR WAY TO COLLEGE"

I watched this happy throng until my secretary came into the room. He said:

"The news of your cabinet selections has already begun to burst upon the country like the news of a declaration of War."

"It is a declaration of war," I said. "It's war against partisanship, sectionalism and class prejudice."

The appointments were entirely unexpected for not even the men I had selected for my Cabinet had the slightest suspicion that they were to be named.

About Senator Borah's acceptance I had no doubt. I knew him as a great public servant, an

[9]

honest man and a man of great courage. He would not hesitate to accept the responsibilities of the State Department, I was certain, and later events proved that my faith was not misplaced.

Soon after I had sent the cabinet names to the Senate, my secretary informed me that Mr. Hoover was trying to get me on the telephone from Palo Alto, California. I had the call transferred to my study and after I had identified myself I heard the voice of that Quaker gentleman say:

"Er-r-r-r, Mr. President—er-r-r, this is Hoover. Is it true that you have tendered me the position of Secretary of Commerce?"

I said I had sent his name to the Senate.

"But, Mr. President, I should have been consulted," the former President said. "This has placed me in a very embarrassing position."

"In what way, Mr. Hoover?" I inquired.

"Why, I am a former President of the United States, and it's a terrible step down for me to be asked to serve in your cabinet," he replied.

"Now let me put you straight," I said. "You say you are being embarrassed because, as a former President of the United States, it would be a step down for you to serve as a cabinet officer under another President. Just what is your position in public life today, Mr. Hoover?"

He hesitated and then:

"Well, suppose I decline any appointment upon the ground that I do not care to be associated with you?" came the now steady tones of the Quaker gentleman.

"All right, Mr. Hoover," I replied. "That is something for you to decide in your own conscience. I shall not attempt to influence you. It is something between you and the American people. You will have to explain to them why you will not serve your country again in its hour of need."

Mr. Hoover's voice lost its angry tone.

"All right, Mr. President," he replied. "I will consider it."

My secretary entered the room as I concluded my talk with Mr. Hoover.

"Governor Smith is here and wants to talk to you," my secretary said. "He looks madder than when he lost the nomination at Chicago."

A moment later, Alfred E. Smith entered the executive office. He wore an overcoat and carried a derby hat in his hand.

"How are you, Governor?" I inquired, speaking first. I arose and held out my hand. My friendly attitude halted the storm of words that he apparently intended to say. He crossed the room and, somewhat hesitantly, shook hands with me.

"How are you, Governor?" I asked again. "You're looking fit."

"I'm feeling fine, thank you," he responded. Then, unable to restrain himself another moment, he ejaculated:

"Say, Huey, what's the big idea?"

"Fine," I replied. "We agree right off the bat."

"What do you mean, agree?" he demanded.

"We agree your appointment as Director of the Budget is a big idea," I informed him. "I think it's better than big; I think it's a grand idea, or I wouldn't have appointed you. Here is your commission."

I handed him the executive order, naming him Director of the Budget. He took the paper and looked at it a moment.

"I can't understand your action," he said. "We've been political enemies for years. Why, in the Roosevelt campaign, I told his managers I wouldn't take the stump for him if they let you go out for him."

"Yes," I retorted, "and long before that I found out what a mistake I had made when I tried to talk the people into electing you President of the United States. I guess I didn't do so badly at that, because if I had recommended Hoover that year, I would have had as much to apologize for."

"And yet you have appointed both Hoover and me?" he inquired wonderingly.

"Not as President, Al,—and not as assistant President, but as men with vision and capacity to administer big jobs."

"It's preposterous," he said. "Do you think my ideas would change toward you? How well do you think you and I would get along together?"

"I've taken a page from your own political career, Al," I continued. "I have studied your record as Governor of New York. I found that you sought out the finest type of men, the best qualified men for the public appointments you made, though once in a while you let political consideration enter into your decisions.

"I want you to know why I named you. I know you are the father of the budget. As Governor of New York, you were the first man in public life to budget the appropriations. After that the Federal government established a budget and created the office of Director of the Budget. So you really are the father of this job."

"Huey, you amaze me," he ejaculated. "I thought you were naming me for the publicity of the thing."

"Well," I said, "I intend asking Congress to

elevate the Director of the Budget to the Cabinet. On top of that, I want you—if you become Director—to undertake to carry out some Democratic campaign pledges and some Republican campaign pledges."

"What pledges are you talking about?"

Picking up a booklet on party platforms, I read from the Republican platform of 1924:

> We demand, and the people of the United States have a right to demand, rigid economy in Government."

Then, turning the pages to the Democratic platform of 1928:

> The Democratic party stands for efficiency and economy in the administration of public affairs, and we pledge:
>
> (a) Businesslike reorganization of all the departments of the Government.
>
> (b) The elimination of duplication, waste and overlapping.
>
> (c) Substitution of modern businesslike methods for existing obsolete and antiquated conditions.

As I read, the Governor removed his overcoat. He smiled as I concluded.

"Well, my old friend, Franklin, forgot that

plank entirely," he observed.

"Yes, but I had it in my platform, and I am going to keep my promise to carry it into effect," I said.

"Huey," Smith said, shaking a finger at me, "I think I've had you wrong all the time."

We shook hands.

As Smith left, Senator Couzens was ushered into my study. He greeted me.

"Well, Huey," he said, "I see you're raising as much hell as President as you did in the Senate."

He soon made me realize that he feared the possibility of disharmony in a cabinet of so many strong-minded men.

"For instance," he asked, "how can Smith and Roosevelt work together? How about Borah and Hoover?"

"What do I care whether they agree with one another?" I asked. "Let Smith run the budget. Hoover will run the Commerce Department to a queen's taste. He will do a mighty fine job there, you'll see. And why should Borah quarrel with Hoover over how Hoover runs the Commerce Department, any more than Hoover will quarrel with Borah about how Borah runs the State Department?"

After he had said he would accept the appointment as Secretary of the Treasury, I told Senator Couzens that I expected a balanced budget and that we must carry out my campaign promise to limit the income of any one man to around $500,-000 per year and limit inheritances to be received by any one person to $1,000,000. He agreed, remarking that the last direction would cost his family a pretty penny.

Before we parted, Senator Couzens undertook the task of communicating with the others I had selected for cabinet posts and urging them to accept. He said he would try to win their consent by reminding them of the national danger through which we were passing.

"Why, your very election is a danger signal," he said frankly.

By dinner time on inauguration day I had received acceptances from Smith, Keating, Murphy and Couzens.

The reporters of the press and radio had waited patiently for me to grant them my first interview. I ordered my secretary to admit them all. I soon acquainted them with all the matters I had handled up to date.

"Now, gentlemen of the press, that's all the news I have for you today, but I would like your advice. I want to get these men to accept posts in

"HELLO! KINGFISH"

my cabinet. What do you advise me to do?"

"Why, Mr. President," replied one of them, "I would make a radio appeal to the country tonight, asking business leaders, political leaders, and the common people to join in asking them to serve."

"That would get Borah and Roosevelt," someone shouted from the rear of the room.

"Splendid," I said. "I'll do just that thing. Thank you a lot for your suggestion. Now, I guess that concludes your first interview."

"One thing more, Mr. President," a reporter asked. "What arrangements shall we have to see you?"

"I understand you have an association here," I said. "I know you boys are patriots as well as reporters. I will follow any arrangement your association decides is proper, bearing in mind, of course, the tremendous work I must do. I will see you when your association is ready to report."

As the reporters made ready to leave I said to them:

"Now, look here! You can help me. I want to avoid being 'yessed' to death."

"That cabinet you've picked will cure that," one remarked.

"But they have their work to do. What I ask is this: Whenever a majority in your association think there is incompetence or bad judgment or a need for me to have some knowledge or opinion you have, let that come to me. I may or may not follow you on various opinions, but give me this contact."

They gave me their promise.

I had been told that former President Franklin D. Roosevelt would leave after the inaugural ceremonies to take a rest on an estate just outside Washington. Some minutes after ten o'clock that night I was called to the telephone.

I heard a voice:

"Hello, Kingfish!"

It was Franklin D. Roosevelt. The last time he called me by that title was in greeting me in a telephone conversation the day before he was nominated for the Presidency by the Democratic convention at Chicago in 1932.

"Yes, Mr. President," I answered.

"What in the world do you mean by offering me a cabinet post, after all the things you have said about me as President?" he demanded.

"I only offered you a position which I thought you were qualified to fill."

"Well, I thank you for the gesture, Huey, but I can't feel that you have complimented me very much."

[18]

"Why not, Frank?"

"Well, it's a terrible fall from the Presidency to the Secretaryship of the Navy," he replied.

"You sound just like Hoover," I said, "but he couldn't call to mind any position he held just now."

"Well, Huey, I'll have to give this more consideration," the former President told me. "I had a statement all prepared here, declining, but I'll destroy it. Say, suppose I accept and fail to become the best Secretary? What's the penalty then?"

"In that case," I replied, "people will hold me responsible, and they may punish me for your failure."

The former President chuckled:

"Well, Huey, that's almost reason enough to accept the position. You'll hear from me later."

It soon became practically certain that all members of the cabinet, as selected, would accept.

My worries about the completion of my cabinet being almost over, I undertook to set in motion my plan for a redistribution of the nation's wealth.

My plan was outlined in my first legislative message to the Congress, which I delivered orally on the second day of my Presidency. In it I recommended the creation of a giant national organization for a survey of all wealth and poverty. It was the first step in carrying out the Share Our Wealth program.

Believing, as I told the assembled House and Senate, that "the people make fewer mistakes than we," I proposed to place in charge of this survey only those people who owed their positions to the votes of the people. It was my view, in which most members of Congress readily concurred, that ultimate power, to be exercised over important governmental functions within the states, should be given only into the hands of persons in whom the people had expressed abiding faith and confidence.

So I proposed to the Congress that the Share Our Wealth survey should be conducted by the Governors of the states, members of the Senate and members of the House of Representatives. My recommendation was that the survey in each state should be conducted by a board of which the senior United States Senator would be chairman, the junior Senator, the Governor, and the members of the House of Representatives, the other members. Each member of the House would serve on the board only on that portion of the survey affecting his own Congressional district.

I further proposed that, in the event of a controversy in which the board failed to reach a conclusion by a majority vote, the legislation should give to the President the power to appoint a personal member to join the board for the purpose of settling the controversy by casting the odd vote.

I proposed that Congress itself lay down the rule by which wealth should be measured, both as to realty values and as to security values.

I proposed that Congress should authorize these state boards, not only to take an inventory of all wealth, but to survey the property within the state to determine to the best of human ability the amount of annual income received by each family earning less than $2,500 a year, which was to be guaranteed them under the Share Our Wealth program. I further asked Congress to authorize these boards to take a census of all families who did not possess a family homestead valued at $5,000.

My message created a sensation. It met with instant approval from the people, who heartily favored the idea of putting their own elected officials in charge of the survey in each state. The people believed that the integrity of the states was being protected when the elected officers of highest trust among them were placed in immediate charge of this work.

II

Wherein We Arrange to Overhaul and Revive the Nation

"Go the whole hog;" dust storms and floods curbed; water supply, power and navigation supplied in all regions; national defense; farm agents handle farm bureaus to restore agricultural life; banks made servants of the people; harmony and revival of all agencies of transportation.

ON my return to the White House, after delivering my message to Congress, I found General Smedley D. Butler, my Secretary of War, and General Lytle Brown, my Secretary of Interior, waiting to see me. I greeted them warmly. It seemed that I understood them more intimately than some of my other appointees to the cabinet.

"Why in the world did you ever pick on me for this job?" were General Brown's first words. "Why, I haven't seen you in years—not since we worked together on the Mississippi River flood control problems."

"Well, General, we have the greatest development project ever known in the whole world," I said. "Your great saying used to be 'Go the whole hog.' We're going it. You know that plan we discussed back there when I was Governor of Louisiana, don't you?"

"Yes, indeed," replied General Brown. "That plan was drafted while I was Chief of Army Engineers, and I started the first work under it. We were going as fast as we could, limited only by the amount of money Congress appropriated for us. The study and the plans are complete."

I picked up a morning newspaper from my desk

and told Brown to read an article on the first page. It was date-lined from a western state, and it told of the great danger of blighting dust storms in the spring, due to lack of heavy snow during the winter months in the mountain and prairie land. It said that unless the west got heavy snows before the middle of March, there would be another terrible dust storm blight in the spring.

"This looks very serious," said General Brown.

"I think so, too," I agreed, "and that is why I am putting you in charge of this vast program for the elimination of dust storms, the reclamation of waste lands, the control of floods, and the development of navigation and water power throughout the entire country."

"You mean we're really going to carry out that ten-billion-dollar engineering program that we drafted while I was Chief of Army Engineers?" Brown inquired.

"Yes, and more," I said, "we will have to enlarge it before we are finished. For instance, you should take the surplus water of the Red River and divert it at North Texas so that it flows through other streams and finally into the Rio Grande. Texas streams need that water. So do their lands."

"Sure, didn't I tell you that, too?"

"Yes, but now I'm telling you."

"How will we proceed?" asked the General.

"It will come under the board of Army Engineers, but the construction will be handled through the Public Works Administration."

"Mr. President," said General Brown, "to save a lot of repetition, General Butler and I had better get hold of General Edward M. Markham, the present Chief of Army Engineers. The three of us can agree on proper plans for initiating this tremendous program."

"You get your plans going, picking your projects with a view to eliminating the menace of dust storms and floods as the first objective. I would like to complete this whole ten-billion-dollar program in five years. That would be at the rate of two billion dollars a year. If feasible, devote the first year's work to the dust storm area, so as to erect a water barrier against dust storms and to furnish water for that part of the country where dust storms arise, and for the sections where the dust storms do the most damage by destroying crops on otherwise fertile land."

"I think that's a very proper way of starting the program, Mr. President," agreed General Brown.

"Now, gentlemen, it may develop that you will have to move whole communities from the arid areas to the sites of dam projects, first to furnish labor for the projects and second, possibly, because even these hardy westerners will be unable to live in the dust storm areas until we are able to control the storms.

"This moving of the people from the arid lands will be your job, General Butler. You take charge of that just as soon as Brown tells you the number of workers he needs on his various projects. You ought to be able to start work on the projects and the moving of the people as soon as the spring thaw arrives.

"Now, Smedley, this will be a great military problem. You know that in both Belgium and France one of the greatest problems in the early days of the war was the evacuation of the civilian population from military areas. We have never had an experience in this country along that line. Now, some day the army might be called upon to evacuate the civilian population eastward over the Rocky Mountains, in the event our western coast were invaded or attacked from the air or by pestilence or disease. We never know what problems these new contrivances and inventions will bring to us. In the moving of these people you will have a great military experience. I want you to file complete records in the archives of the War Department, particularly in relation to every mistake you make, and you will make plenty, so your plans can be corrected in the event some future government were faced with the same problem in time of war."

"You certainly are creating a problem which will be of great military importance," said General Butler. "I am eager to start work at once."

Turning to General Brown, he inquired:

"How many projects are there in this ten-billion-dollar program?"

General Brown replied:

"There are 1,600 individual projects, including navigation improvements, reservoirs, levees, irrigation, and dams, scattered through virtually every state in the Union. The primary purpose of this whole program is to control floods, improve navigation, provide water for irrigation, and, incidentally, create power projects."

"How many of these projects are in the drought areas?"

"Well, there are eight reservoirs to be built in Montana, besides fifteen irrigation projects. In Wyoming there will be six reservoirs and about thirteen irrigation projects. In Nebraska there will be eight more reservoirs and ten irrigation projects. In Colorado there will be two great reservoirs and seven new irrigation projects. In

Kansas there will be five reservoirs and many flood control projects. There will be fourteen reservoirs and numerous flood control projects in Oklahoma, while Texas has ten reservoirs. In the east, the plan includes reservoirs, dams and navigation improvements in every state from Maine to Florida."

"We took the money of our western taxpayers to help save us from the flood waters that came from their rivers. Now we are going out to these people who are our partners, and not only give them back some of their money, but also give them back some of their water.

"Don't you think you had better announce this plan pretty soon?" I asked. "They are badly discouraged out there by the dust storms of the last three years, and the grave menace of similar storms in the future."

"These maps and the whole plan can be published at once," said General Brown. "I understand on some of the land the dust has blown so thick that, unless the area is properly watered, it will be many years before the land can be cultivated again. Of course, this dust is rich top soil, and a few heavy rains might make another story of it."

General Butler interrupted us.

[30]

"How does this program prevent dust storms?" he inquired.

General Brown replied:

"The idea is to retain the flood waters of these various western levees in the mountains, up near the head waters of each stream. In the past the spring freshets and floods have roared in torrents down the rivers, causing tremendous floods and great damage in the lower part of each of these rivers, washing away top soil and robbing the upper country of its water supply. If we build a string of reservoirs near the head waters of these western streams, we will retain tremendous supplies of water in the mountains.

"The trouble in the dust storm area of the west has been that the countryside got no rain. It couldn't very well get rain when even the mountains were dry. We believe that these huge reservoirs in the hills will supply a source of rain, in addition to permitting the construction of thousands of irrigation projects in sections which did not get rain even in normal periods."

"Will Congress appropriate the necessary money?"

"There is no question about that," I replied. "By the time you have completed your project, the wealth of America will have been increased by not less than some 50 to 100 billions of dollars, and the people employed in the meantime. Besides that, we can pay for it either by general taxation or from our Share Our Wealth program. You need not worry about the cost. The American people will be far more eager to spend ten billion dollars on this wealth-giving and farsighted program than it was to squander billions on the hit-or-miss programs of the last administration."

Both Generals arose. As I shook hands with General Butler, I said:

"Now, Smedley, we've got lots of cobwebs to sweep out of the War Department. Of course, it is a wonderful institution, but you know there must be a number of things changed. I know something about military aviation, and I think we must reorganize and modernize our air forces."

"All right," said General Butler, "That suits me fine. I'm a soldier and not a legislator."

FARM PROBLEM

A meeting of farmers' representatives was held at the public auditorium in Washington, to discuss plans and details for carrying out the government's farm program.

The appointment of the Secretary of Agriculture proved to be of general delight to the gathering.

INAUGURATION

The meeting had been in session only a short time before those in the farm organization service, due to farmers' selections and their confidence in them, were placed in the government's farm bureau to take the management helm away from the chronic bureaucrats who, for 20 years, had brought wreckage to agriculture under all presidents.

The farm policy was well understood. The Secretary in his address to the gathering said:

> Gentlemen, the underlying basis for all our plan is the cost of production and a living for the farmer in respectable circumstances. Our plan, and the general government plan, takes care of that. I would not connect myself to this work unless it meant that much to our people.
>
> We will not go to these bureaus to try to teach them something about farm problems; we will be the bureau hereafter. We can work together now as we have, only no one will be in our way. Laws? There is only one law to cover it all. It is the law Moses gave us from the lips of the Lord. When it fails, I'm ready to fail with it.
>
> We have much building to do to make facilities ready to store our surplus products. Mind you, if we ever get very far ahead and store up enough to last awhile, the govern-

ment will use us for other work until consumption catches up with our production. But hereafter, the government will always keep a surplus, if it can get enough products to do so, in order to prepare for any emergency or distress that may threaten.

As the meeting adjourned Mr. Kennedy, Secretary of the Farmers' Union, grabbed my arm and said:

"Here, Huey, you have said so much about bureaucrats and now you have turned me into one; does that mean I cannot see you any more?"

"Not until every farmer and farm mother and farm child is happy," I answered.

"Watch us," smiled Kennedy.

BANKING

The next great problem I considered was that of reforming the federal banking system. Under the leadership of my predecessor, Congress had reformed the powers of the Federal Reserve Board. While leaving private bankers in nominal control, it actually gave the President a great increase in power over the operation of the system.

In my campaign I had pledged the enactment of the banking reform act advocated by Father Charles E. Coughlin of Detroit. I was determined to carry that pledge into effect.

The Secretary of the Treasury, aware of my intentions, telephoned me one day, shortly after the inauguration, asking an appointment to discuss my banking program. I told him to come over to the White House at once.

On his arrival, he said:

"Mr. President, do you intend to ask Congress to enact the Coughlin banking bill?"

"I do," I told him. "Have you any objections to it?"

"None to the idea of a popular control of the banking system through elected officers. There are numerous minor provisions of the Coughlin bill which has been introduced in past Congresses, which must be revised for the purpose of clarity, and to make the new system foolproof."

"Then we are in accord, Mr. Secretary," I said, "because I am finally convinced that we will never get a private banking system in this or any other country to provide proper credit facilities for our people and to insure a banking structure safe against all the ravages of changing economic conditions. Private banking, as such, has failed in every emergency in every country in the world. How it can be defended any longer is beyond me. On the other hand, politically controlled banking systems, operated in response to the whim of every new administration, also have failed, and even those systems which political administrations and private bankers controlled jointly, have proved unsatisfactory. I think it is time for us to try out the central bank idea, and to have that central bank controlled by directors elected directly by the people. After all, the people make fewer mistakes than those which can be charged to private bankers."

"The Coughlin bill," said Couzens, "would authorize a board of forty-eight directors, one to be elected in each state. After the board was created, one-sixth of the directors would be elected every two years. They would serve for twelve-year terms."

I replied:

"I am in accord on the election of these directors, one from each state, but I would like you to consider whether it would be better to elect one-third of the board every two years, and fix the terms at six years, just as members of the Senate are elected. It seems to me twelve-year terms are a little long, and I believe it would be better to have every member of the board go back to the people of his state for vindication of his conduct of that office every sixth year instead of every twelfth year."

[36]

"I believe you're right, Mr. President."

"Now, where does this Coughlin plan differ from the proposals made by the private bankers?" I inquired.

"Except in minor details, the main objection of private bankers to the Coughlin bill has been that it takes control of the banking system out of their hands and gives it to persons elected by the people," replied Couzens, "The bankers call that political control of banking."

"So it is a purely superficial objection, isn't it?"

"Exactly, Mr. President," replied Couzens. "You know bankers; they love power. They haven't been content to run their banks; they have used the resources of the people, the deposits of their customers, and their control of credit, to acquire a dominant control over transportation, industry, and all manner of commerce. They know that, once they lose control of the banking system, they will lose their present control of transportation, industry and commerce. Their opposition to this sort of legislation is the most unpatriotic, greedy, and heartlessly selfish thing in America today."

"So, anyway you look at it, the Coughlin plan couldn't be as bad as what we have already had from the private bankers?"

"Never," replied Couzens, "and it has the possibilities of providing a really adequate banking system—safe, sound and yet controlled by the people themselves."

"All right, then, Mr. Secretary, I'll draft a message to Congress and we'll ask for the bill's early enactment into law."

TRANSPORTATION

The transportation problem, with its tremendous effect on the life and happiness of the American people, through its relation to the cost of distributing food and other supplies, was called to my attention in rather startling fashion during the early days of my administration. The very latest development in streamline trains established a new transcontinental record from Chicago to the west coast. I heard from Secretary of Labor Keating for the first time after his appointment when he telephoned me to boast of the record.

I told him I planned to call a conference to determine a transportation policy to improve the condition of our railroads and to reduce the cost of distribution, especially of farm products, if that were possible. I told him to extend my invitation to the Secretary of the Treasury, the Attorney General, the Secretary of Agriculture, Joseph B.

Eastman, Federal Co-ordinator of Transportation
and to Senator William Gibbs McAdoo, to confer
with me later in the day on this great problem.

When the gentlemen assembled in my office that
afternoon, I told them I hoped we would be able
to agree upon a program for bringing order out of
chaos in the transportation industry, to reduce the
cost of transporting foodstuffs as a means of reducing the cost of living, and to perfect a transportation policy which would protect the railroads
from the ruinous practises of their competitors. I
asked for comment.

Attorney General Murphy was the first to
speak.

"I have always been for government ownership
of railroads," he said. "If any great social problem, such as a food shortage, should overtake our
people, the railroads, under government ownership,
could solve it in a far more brilliant way than they
could under private control. There is no question
in my mind about that."

"Well, gentlemen, if we decide to purchase the
roads, we must decide, too, how we shall pay for
them. Shall we pay by exchanging government
bonds for railroad securities?" Turning to Mr.
Eastman, I inquired, "What's the total value of
outstanding railroad securities?"

"Probably something above ten billion dollars," Eastman replied. "Back in 1929 the market value of all steam railway securities was over $22,000,-000,000, but about $10,000,000,000 of that has been wiped out in market losses since the crash. In fact, in 1933, the total value of railway securities was less than $9,000,000,000, but there has been some recovery in that market since then."

"Well, you gentlemen must decide whether we are to pay their market value or fix their value in some other way, if we decide to make the purchase."

"That would be a very important question," said McAdoo. "I should say, offhand, that we should consider four factors in determining the value of any railroad. First would be its reconstruction value new, less depreciation; second would be its stock and bond value; third, its earning value, and fourth, its true worth, or the value of its services. One way we could decide that occurs to me offhand as being very fair, both to the American people who would be the purchasers and to the holders of railway securities, will be to pay the sum of one-fourth of each of these four values."

Secretary Couzens spoke up for the first time:

"Mr. President, have you ever considered the advisability of an outright subsidization of the rail-

roads in return for absolute government control,
as an alternative to outright government ownership? We subsidize the railroads now through
mail contracts, and we have some control over
roads through the Interstate Commerce Commission."

"Well, Jim," I interrupted him, "you know I
want every water carrier that is using these rivers
and harbors (developed and maintained by federal
funds) to have the help of the government, which
means we must have some control over them so as
to coordinate all transportation and have it survive. That is one thing we must do, no matter
what we do about the purchase of railroads. But
what are your suggestions?"

"I had in the back of my head, Mr. President,
an idea that, whether we purchased the roads or
openly subsidized them in return for absolute federal control, we might do away with a lot of the
injustices of transportation costs by arranging a
rate schedule similar to the postal rate schedule.
You know, we carry a letter from Washington to
Baltimore for three cents, but we carry another
letter of the same weight and size from Washington to Seattle for the same rate. Our parcel post
rates are by zones, according to weight. We might
give some products, such as foodstuffs, the letter

rate, while imposing the parcel post rate on all other commodities. We could adjust rates according to seasons when particular foodstuffs are moving to markets."

The meeting could last no longer.

"Now, gentlemen, in parting, I want you to carry away a final idea," I told them. "If government ownership of the railroads is the proper solution of our transportation problem, recommend it to me. If outright subsidy and absolute government control is the answer, recommend that. In either case, I want to reduce the cost of transporting food, so we can reduce the cost of living. In either case, I want the railroads free from a competition which benefits by indirect federal subsidy, which in turn the railroads have to help to pay, and I want motor bus lines and water carriers brought under control, side by side with the railroads. We must live and let live, modernize and advance for them all."

III

Wherein We Care for the Soul and Body of a Great Nation

*We send every boy and girl
to college; humanity given
the care to avoid crime;
curbing the flames; the lives
of the living.*

We go to School:

PROCLAMATION

TO MY FELLOW CITIZENS, THE AMERICAN PEOPLE:

One hundred and forty-eight years ago, the people of the United States began a new form of government on this continent, "in order to form a more perfect Union, establish Justice, insure domestic Tranquility, provide for the common defense, promote the general Welfare, and secure the Blessings of Liberty to ourselves and our Posterity."

Today extreme inequalities in the distribution of wealth have closed the doors of opportunity to millions of our children.

Education is a function which the states can handle adequately only if helped by the federal government, and the government ought to see that such benefits of education are extended to all classes of citizens; but here in our beloved America we find inequalities in the benefits of the public schools. Some children are given excellent educational facilities in great, sanitary buildings with ample equipment, with well-fed, well-trained teachers. Other children have poor educational facilities, unsanitary buildings, meager equipment,

[45]

untrained, poorly-paid teachers. The bitter fruits of these inequalities of opportunity, which endure for generations, must and shall be corrected.

Therefore we, the Government of the United States, do hereby proclaim a policy to the people of the United States, that this Government shall extend aid, financial and idealistic, to the several states, so that every worthy boy and girl, every worthy man and woman, may secure an education to the limit of their mental capacity, so that teachers and instructors may receive an adequate income, thereby gaining their God-given right to an equal enjoyment of the blessings of American liberty.

Given this Fourth day of February, in the year of our Lord One Thousand Nine Hundred Thirty-Seven, and in the year of our Independence, the One Hundred Sixty-first.

HUEY PIERCE LONG,
President of the United States.

After writing out this proclamation, I summoned to my office the Assistant Secretary of the Interior, Oscar L. Chapman, and Dr. John W. Studebaker, Commissioner of Education. When they arrived I handed them the proclamation to read. Chapman read it over Studebaker's shoulder.

"Well," said Chapman, when they had finished reading, "just what shall we say this means? What shall we do?"

"It means," I answered, "that I am writing a letter to the fathers and mothers of the United States to say:

"*'I will send your boy and girl to college.'*

"And we are to increase the United States financial aid to the states for the operation of all schools, with a new federal aid fund for the states to furnish a college education for every boy and girl, able to pass the entrance examinations but denied the blessings of a college education by a lack of money," I told them. "I want you, Mr. Chapman, to take charge of this program for me, because construction funds will be required and the problem goes far beyond the mere classroom. I want you, Mr. Studebaker, to take charge of the educational side, and I know you two gentlemen will cooperate with each other where your duties overlap."

Both men nodded endorsement.

"And the first thing we must do is raise the salaries of teachers and instructors to a level which equals their duties, responsibilities and training," I added.

Dr. Studebaker looked at me and said:

"One in every three of our teachers is receiving less than $750 a year."

"Why, up at the Capitol we pay that much to Senate pages who have to be under fourteen years of age," I said. "I want your Commission to determine a decent living salary scale for the teachers in all schools benefitting from federal funds. To me it is just as important to have our schools manned by prosperous and qualified teachers as to have them filled with happy, healthy youngsters.

"But that is only part of it," I continued. "Since my plan to share our wealth insures every family enough to sustain life and educate their children, there ought not to be many cases where the children cannot study or train in college. However, see to it that our plan leaves no boy or girl without the choice of attending college, regardless of the means of the student or the parents.

"Then," I concluded, "see to it that there is a system of standards so that the student, during study and training, will be ushered into the line of education or training for which his capacities show him to be best fitted."

"Sure," answered Chapman, "there is need for both the blacksmith and the lawyer. Good training and hours of work make the pursuit of one

"NO MAN SHOULD HAVE TO BECOME A CRIMINAL . . ."

calling as delightful as the other. You want us not to divert the legally inclined mind toward the calling of a blacksmith, or vice versa."

"Exactly," I answered. "And further, let us secure coordination to try and turn out in each line of endeavor something like the proportion a nation will need."

"I thoroughly agree with you, Mr. President," said Dr. Studebaker, and Chapman nodded his head in corroboration.

"Our founding fathers made the provision for the permanent endowment and development of common school education," said Dr. Studebaker. "You know, Mr. President, even before the Constitution was adopted, the Continental Congress, by the ordinance of May 20, 1785, prepared the way for the advance of settlements and for the development of public education as contemporaneous projects. This ordinance reserved four lots out of each township in any new territory acquired by the United States, to be set aside for the maintenance of public schools within the said townships. It was an educational endowment of 640 acres of land in every new township. It was the first federal subsidy for education. The ordinance did not mention the manner in which public schools were to be established; it merely laid down a principle which finally dedicated not less than 1/36th of all public lands, with certain exceptions as to mineral rights, to the cause of education by public schools."

"Yes," I said. "I recall that in the ordinance of July 13, 1787, for the government of the territory of the United States northwest of the Ohio River, Congress declared:

> Religion, morality and knowledge being necessary to good government and the happiness of mankind, schools and the means of education shall forever be encouraged.

"What a marvelous set of men they were, our founding fathers. They held that religion, morality and knowledge were necessary to good government and the happiness of mankind. That epitomizes the platform on which I was elected to the Presidency."

* * *

Crime and Punishment:

The first serious talk I had with my Attorney General convinced me I had chosen the man among a million for the post. As we shook hands in my executive office I felt his piercing eyes boring into my soul. I knew instantly that Frank Murphy was reading my heart and mind

as though they were open books, and that something he sensed in me seemed to satisfy him.

I said to him:

"Frank, there are thousands, possibly tens of
thousands, of people walking the streets today,
their pockets bulging with ill-gotten gain, who
should be in jail for economic crimes. But there
must be thousands, possibly tens of thousands,
of people in jail, who should be free. I mean
there are fathers of families, who stole a loaf of
bread, or a bottle of milk, or a pig, or broke into
a store to get canned goods to keep their wives
and children from starving to death in this great
economic crisis, and were punished with as heart-
less a cruelty as was ever displayed by Roman
tyrants against the early Christians. How can
we get them out of jail? I am willing to pardon
every one of those cases where the prisoners are
in federal jails, convicted of that type of crime;
but what about the state prisoners in state jails?"

"There can be no two rules about that, Mr.
President, but we must be very discriminating if
we are to be sensible in dealing with that problem,"
the Attorney General replied. "Men who committed crime to furnish food for their children
should not have been punished in the first place.
In fact, they should have been treated with

sympathy for having dared a prison sentence in order to feed their children.

"I feel a board should be instituted in every state of the Union, to be composed of psychiatrists and sociologists, with a competent person to represent the public at large. I would have such boards review every case called to their attention, in which the man serving the sentence has been convicted of a crime committed under the driving urge of self-preservation. In every case where there was no previous record, and where there are women and children dependent upon the prisoner for livelihood, I would release him.

"I understand, General, that crime is costing our country twelve billion dollars—I mean twelve hundred million dollars—annually," I said.

"That's correct," he replied. "And besides, we spend about forty million dollars a year on the prosecution of federal crimes alone. The cost of punishing crime is a drop in the bucket compared to the actual crime loss. Obviously, if we spend a billion dollars a year to eliminate crime—instead of a mere fifty million, or some few hundred millions in all the country—and thereby cut our crime loss in half, we would save five or six billion dollars a year to the American people."

"Again we agree," I said. "But how should we

approach this problem of reducing crime?"

"It should begin in childhood, in our public and private schools," the Attorney General replied. "Our school children should be taught a greater respect for law, not only in the schools but in the homes. There should be a revival of religious training in the home, without regard to faith, but in keeping with uplifting teachings. There should be a complete reorganization of our correctional institutions to which we send the boy and girl who makes a single mistake."

"I shall charge you, as Attorney General, with that responsibility and that duty," I told him. "You shall set an example in federal institutions and we shall educate state administrations, through publicity and whatever influence we have, to follow your example, wherever they have not done so heretofore on their own initiative."

"You make me very happy, Mr. President, by giving me such a duty," he replied.

"Now, shouldn't there be some reformation or revision of our judicial methods of meting out punishment?" I next inquired.

"Mr. President, you have touched a subject with which I have had practical experience, and on which I have very pronounced views," he replied. "The present method of issuing sentences in our federal and state courts is a disgrace to the name of Justice."

"Oh, yes, you have been a judge yourself," I said. "What are your suggestions on that score?"

"I believe," said the Attorney General, "that every man should be sentenced only on the recommendation of a sociologist and psychiatrist. They should have before them a social, economic, moral, and mental picture of the man, as well as knowledge of the circumstances of the crime, before ever imposing a sentence. They should understand his career from childhood, some facts about his conduct in school, and his record, if any, in private employment.

"We cling to the idea of punitive justice, instead of an intelligent and critical judgment of a crime based upon the social, moral and economic facts of his case. We want to punish, and not to correct conditions by using common sense in administering justice. It is a sadistic strain in our system.

"It took a second of my time for me, when I was a judge, to impose a life sentence. But it took a life-time from that man. Sometimes such sentences are imposed by ignorance, and sometimes by laziness, and sometimes by mere indigestion in the judge."

[54]

"You believe, then, there should be a sentencing board in every federal court, to sentence intelligently, after compiling an accurate record of the man's life?" I asked.

"Yes. And that record should go to the penal board, so that, if and when the man is sentenced, the penal authorities may deal with him intelligently, in accord with the recommendations of the sociologists and psychiatrists who have joined in sentencing him."

"You believe, then, that such a record would enable the penal boards to prescribe the correct treatment in prisons for the redemption of the criminal?"

"Exactly," said the Attorney General. "I feel we must reorganize the present system of operating our jails. We must isolate first offenders and prevent them absolutely from associating with hardened criminals. It is such associations that place the first offender beyond redemption under our present system. We must make efforts to reclaim the hardened criminal. I know of cases where the veteran offender was committing crime undoubtedly because he had the mentality of a nine-year-old and the fundamental education of a child of about the same age."

"I agree with you," I said, and continued:

"Now, General, we ought to do something to help the fire departments. We ought to give them some help along the line that we are going to help police departments. You know, Frank, we are losing 10,000 lives and hundreds of millions of dollars each year, in fires. It seems that the Federal government ought to take some recognition of this fearful loss of life and property."

"Certainly," said the Attorney General. "I had thought the Bureau of Standards was conducting experiments and helping fire departments."

"Just a little, but it is handicapped by lack of funds," I told him. "During the campaign I was talking to a fire chief. He told me that Federal Fire Council was doing splendid service, but that there was need for a new agency or for an expansion of activities at the Bureau of Standards. The Bureau, he said, makes tests of fire resisting and fire protecting materials, but improvements in fire-fighting apparatus is a sort of 'error and correction' affair. I understand that the Baltimore department invented a hydrant connection some time ago for use by departments that operate with only a single piece of apparatus in each company, and that here in Washington they invented a cellar syphon to use in drawing water out of cellars of homes after the fire has been extinguished. Up in New York City they've invented a dozen practical fire-fighting appliances. It seems to me this sort of problem could be turned over to the Bureau of Standards to solve, instead of having our departments work out such problems for themselves.

"It may be that we can establish a scientific fire school here or, if that is not appropriate, at least we can establish an agency to collect data from various fire departments and departmental fire schools, and disseminate it through the country. Consult with the Federal Fire Council and the Association of Fire Underwriters, and the heads of some of our fire departments, and the Science Advisory Board, and bring me a plan for giving greater federal aid to fire departments."

"I will be glad to, Mr. President," said the Attorney General.

"Now, General, we will need legislation from Congress to do all these things. You bring me a complete legislative program, and I shall join you in asking Congress to give us the necessary funds and to enact the necessary laws. Perhaps we will be able to take the blindfold from the eyes of Justice."

The Attorney General arose.

"Mr. President, we shall restore Justice in

America."

"Here," I said, "is my hand upon that."

* * *

Lives Given for the Lives of Others

Late one night, shortly after my inauguration, my secretary brought me a small package. It was a very old book.

As I opened it, a note fluttered to the floor. I picked it up and read:

Dear Huey:

Many years ago you gave this volume to my brother. Won't you write your name in it again, with the date, all in your own handwriting and return it to me?

As ever,
Jim.

I glanced at the volume. It was labelled: "Duty." I thumbed through several pages and finally reached a chapter which began:

A Captain of Dragoons was ordered out with his troop to forage for provisions. They reached a poor cabin and knocked at the door. An old man with a white beard appeared. "Take me to a field," said the officer, "where I can obtain forage for my troops." "Immediately, Sir," replied the old man. He put himself at their head and ascended the valley. After about half an hour's march a fine field of barley appeared. "This will do admirably," said the officer. "No," said the old man, "wait a little, and all will be right." They went on again, until they reached another field of barley. The troops dismounted, mowed down the grain, and trussing it up in bundles, put it up on their horses. "Friend," said the officer, "how is it that you have brought us so far? The first field of barley that we saw was quite as good as this." "That is quite true," said the peasant, "but it was not mine."

"Are there such people living today?" was a question that appeared instantaneously.

A name came into my mind—*MAYO!*

After saving and remaking the lives of thousands, the celebrated Mayo brothers had turned their accumulated earnings to the cause of humanity saying they preferred their children to make their way in the world rather than to become indolent.

I called my secretary.

"Please get one of the Mayo brothers on the telephone. I presume they are at their sanitarium in Rochester, Minnesota."

In a few moments my phone rang and a voice

said: "This is William Mayo. I am at your service, Mr. President."

"I would like you and your brother to come here to Washington to see me whenever you can conveniently make the trip," I informed him.

"What day, Mr. President?" he asked.

"Any time that suits your convenience. I am here all the time."

A few days later I was thrilled when my secretary escorted the Mayo brothers into my office.

"I can't thank you half enough for coming here," I told them.

We shook hands and they drew up chairs beside my desk.

"Gentlemen, I wish to give you a few new patients," I said.

"That is very nice of you, Mr. President," said the elder brother, William J. Mayo. "Some of your friends or members of your family?"

"Well, some of them are my friends," I replied. "Your new patients are to be 130,000,000 people, living in the United States and called Americans. I would like to have you prescribe for them the preventive measures and curative, medicinal treatments which they need. I would like you to help me in stamping out a number of diseases that take

a terrific toll of human life and human effort
from the American people every year. I intend
to have the federal government provide the facilities and equipment which you will need to carry
out this work."

"Why, Mr. President, you startle us," the elder
Mayo replied. "Just how far would you ask us
to go?"

"I want you to go just as far as medical science
will permit you to go," I replied. "I want you
to form a committee of your own profession to
help you. You gentlemen understand the business of organizing, and I shall leave those details
to you."

"But, Mr. President, I would like you to outline a little more clearly just what you have in
mind," the elder Mayo said.

"Well, first," I said, "I would like to enlarge,
under your supervision, the present, insignificant
federal laboratory here in Washington into the
finest laboratory on the face of the globe. I should
like its scientific experimental work extended to in-
clude every known disease for which there is not
a known cause or a satisfactory cure or preventive."

"Why, that is an enormous task, Mr. President," the younger man, Charles H. Mayo, inter-

posed.

"Not enormous to the Government of the United States," I replied. "We have a Government here which has not hesitated to spend billions of dollars and sacrifice hundreds of thousands of lives to kill human beings in other lands, under the sacred name of war. As President of the United States, I shall not hesitate a second to spend millions, or even hundreds of millions of dollars, to kill germs that prey upon the human race, and to war against disease.

" You will need chemists, physicists, pharmacologists, pathologists, gynecologists, immunologists, physiologists and physicians. I hope that you confer with the experts of the Rockefeller Foundation, such as Dr. Simon Flexner; with the scientists of the Carnegie Institute, the scientists of the life insurance companies, and some of our noted research specialists of city laboratories, such as Dr. William H. Parke, of New York City."

"You have given us a task of magnificent prospects, despite its magnitude," said one of the startled brothers.

"I am furnishing you and our people with an opportunity to do something about it and all these other problems of life and death," I replied.

"Well, gentlemen, I wonder whether it isn't possible to discover a real antidote to narcotics and a means of curing the dope addict. I know that these addicts go through a sort of cure; our hospitals and our prisons try to cure them, and they do rid their patients of the immediate habit so that they can live in mental comfort without requiring the exhilaration of narcotics; but inevitably the addict returns to his former habit, as soon as medical vigilance is relaxed."

"I never believe that anything is impossible to the medical profession," the elder Mayo interposed.

"I wonder whether you will undertake the mission of trying to discover new methods for the treatment and cure of the various forms of insanity?" I asked.

"Curing poverty, hunger and nakedness will cure and prevent most of the human ailments," said the elder Mayo.

"Well, gentlemen, would an initial appropriation of five million dollars be enough to start this war on disease?" I asked.

"Oh, yes, but won't we need some authority to act?"

"I shall arrange that."

The two brothers arose.

"We must return to our sanitarium and prepare for an unlimited leave of absence," said the elder Mayo. "I am quite sure our associates will be able to carry on there in our absence. In the meantime, we will consult with the gentlemen and institutions you suggested, and we will be back here in a month ready to go to work and to remain indefinitely. I trust, Mr. President, you will be ready then to have us begin this tremendous work."

"I certainly shall," I replied.

They took their departure and left with me the presentiment that these two, fine, upstanding men would lead the American people out of the wilderness of disease.

After the Mayos left, I sent for the Surgeon General of the United States, Dr. Hugh S. Cumming, head of the Bureau of Public Health Service. When he arrived I told him of my interview with the Mayos and my plans for a great Federal Hygienic Laboratory. He was enthusiastic over the prospect and immediately offered to resign his own post so that one of the Mayos might take it and thereby be in control of the whole Public Health Service. I declined to permit this.

"Oh, no, General Cumming," I told him, "I

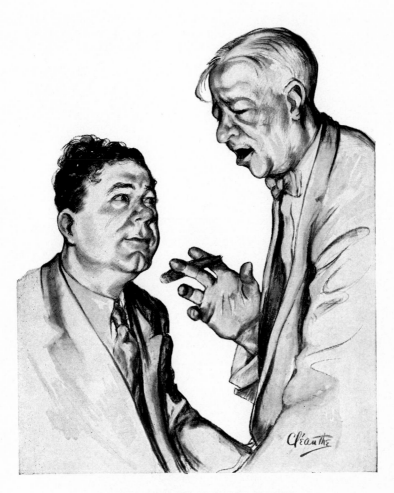

"HUEY, WHAT'S THE BIG IDEA?"

have an equally important task for you to perform as Surgeon General. I only want you to give the Mayos and their appointees a completely free hand in the operation of this laboratory."

"You didn't need to tell me, Mr. President," said the Surgeon General. "I am so enthusiastic about your program that I'd even serve as an interne, just to help the Mayos."

I commended his attitude.

"Now, here's another task: I would like to standardize the education and instruction of nurses. They serve in the trenches of the war against disease. The Government should help to equip them properly for that war. Unless you would have someone else in mind, I might suggest that you consult with Dr. Claude W. Munger, of Valhalla, New York, Chairman of the Nursing Committee of the American Hospital Association, and with Dr. C. E. A. Winslow, Professor of Public Health at Yale. It may be we can recommend new standards for the nursing schools.

"And another thing: I want you to draft a program for educating the public, not only in what we discover at the Laboratory, but in what we already know. Talk to my old friend, Dr. Copeland—you know, Senator Royal S. Copeland —about this phase of the program. He has carried on, almost single-handed, a battle for years to educate the common people in the most simple of medical truths. I want you to confer with him and agree on a program—how we can disseminate authentic medical information quickly, accurately and effectively to the people, in language all can understand."

"I am only too happy to undertake these assignments, Mr. President," the Surgeon General said.

As he departed, I knew the federal government, for the first time in all American History, would care for the health of the American people.

IV

Wherein the New President Encounters the Masters of Finance and Destiny

The ultimatum of J. P. Morgan; the President's answer to Morgan; the conference with Mellon, Aldrich, Dupont, Ford and other financiers; the elder Rockefeller's support; the President's ultimatum for a limit on fortunes.

ONE morning shortly after the inauguration my secretary handed me a letter which had been delivered to the White House by special messenger. It was from J. Pierpont Morgan, the New York capitalist and international banker. The letter read:

JOHN PIERPONT MORGAN
Glen Cove, New York

January 27, 1937.

My dear Mr. President:

I and some of my associates regard your effort to decentralize wealth through the confiscation of individual fortunes in excess of five million dollars, gradually to be reduced even below that to something less than two million dollars, as one of the most autocratic governmental undertakings ever attempted in this or any other civilized country. We regard it not only as an effort to confiscate wealth, but as the first step in changing the economic order upon which all American progress has rested in the past.

We cannot lose sight of the fact that private capital has been the backbone of American progress in industry, commerce and trade. To seize it by governmental decree, we believe to be a violation of the fundamental

[69]

guaranties of the American Constitution.

We are eager as individuals and good citizens to help our American government restore prosperity, provide ease and comfort for all our citizens through the orderly and constitutional processes laid down by our forefathers, but we shall resist any and every unconstitutional effort to seize the wealth, created by individual achievement in a wholly lawful and constitutional manner.

We believe that a full and free opportunity must be preserved in this country to win the traditional reward of superlative individual achievement, whether that reward be counted in hundreds of dollars or hundreds of millions of dollars. We do not express an opinion now as to the advisability or constitutionality of a revenue law limiting the size of fortunes to be accumulated in the future. We content ourselves now with protesting against a law which would take from American citizens, in defiance of their constitutional rights, fortunes already accumulated.

We believe it fitting and proper for the federal government to impose inheritance taxes and estate taxes as a means of providing revenue, but we are forced, Mr. President, to resist in the courts your proposal to seize property outright, without due process of law.

With the highest respect for your office, we feel compelled to notify you that we shall utilize every protection of the courts and Constitution to protect our properties against the seizures contemplated in your Share Our Wealth program.

Very truly yours,
(Signed) J. P. MORGAN.

Honorable Huey Pierce Long,
President of the United States,
The White House,
Washington, D. C.

This threat from the dean of Wall Street's international bankers was the first sign of revolt against the Share Our Wealth program. I welcomed his declaration of war.

Calling a stenographer, I dictated the following reply:

THE WHITE HOUSE

January 28, 1937

My dear Mr. Morgan:

I am in receipt of your letter alleging that the Share Our Wealth program is unconstitutional, and announcing that you will resist its execution in the courts of the land. You are entirely within your rights in pursuing such a course.

I trust upon reflection you will perceive

[71]

that I was the genuine defender of your wealth when I proposed a five million dollar limitation (gradually to be reduced below two million dollars) upon family fortunes in the Share Our Wealth plank of the platform upon which I was elected President of the United States. I will undertake sincerely to carry out the promise by which I secured my election. You are aware, or you would be if you had kept in touch with the sentiment of our American people, that there has been a good deal of whispered complaint against my plan on the ground that it is unjust to permit men of your kind to retain so much as five million dollars of wealth.

In the last campaign you will recall I was bitterly assailed by some speakers for not limiting wealth to one million dollars for each family. In the few days I have occupied the White House, there have been some newspaper editorial comment and numerous "letters from the people" published on editorial pages, demanding a reduction in the five million dollar limit of the Share Our Wealth program to a million dollar maximum at once.

One editorial that I hold in my hand asks this question:

"Why should anyone desiring justice start by proposing such rank inequalities between human beings, all of whom de-

IN THE WHITE HOUSE

serve the equal blessings of God and of government?"

Before me is another newspaper in which a letter is published containing the following sentence:

"Is not our President making a mistake in starting his redistribution of wealth by allowing one family to have one thousand times as much share of the wealth as other families are permitted?"

If you observe the signs about us, my dear Mr. Morgan, you will see that the insignificant quantity of such muttering at this time is insignificant only because our American people as a whole believe they will secure happiness and the comforts of life through the limits placed on huge fortunes by the platform on which I was elected. I concede that my allowances were probably much too high, but I nonetheless told the American people that we could care for all of them bountifully and yet allow men of wealth such as yourself fortunes of about five million dollars, until gradually reduced below two million dollars. I also told them that we would limit fortunes only to the point necessary to guarantee comfort, convenience and education to the balance of our people.

I have felt that this moderated program,

which allowed enough wealth to any family to inspire effort, service and achievement, but proposed such a limit as would curb needless greed, would create a proper balance between wealth and poverty, thereby insuring the maximum of inspiration to all our people. That being the case, I anticipate no difficulty from the common people of our country in securing to you the maximum limit of five million dollars of wealth, which the Share Our Wealth program would permit you to wholly own and manage in your own name until gradually reduced.

I am surprised, naturally, that as a banker and business man of reputed sagacity, you do not realize that my program is a real benefit to you. In my campaign for the Presidency I promised a return to Constitutional government. Needless to say, I am convinced the capital tax levies are constitutional. If they had not been, this republic could have never begun. I concede, too, that men may differ with me on this legal question. I therefore shall be content to permit a test of its constitutionality in the Supreme Court of the United States before carrying it generally into effect.

We are about to engage upon a governmental survey of wealth and of the requisites of our common people for their comfort,

convenience and education. When that is
completed, Congress will reassemble and will
enact the Share Our Wealth program. If in
the meantime you should have a change of
heart, Mr. Morgan, on the wisdom of resisting this equitable redistribution of wealth, I
shall be only too happy to have you volunteer
your services in helping to carry this program
quietly into effect without needless disturbance of business, commerce or industry.

Very truly yours,
HUEY PIERCE LONG.

Mr. J. Pierpont Morgan,
Glen Cove, N. Y.

I said to my stenographer:
"Send copies of that letter to the following
men:

John D. Rockefeller, Jr., 10 West 54th Street,
New York City;

Henry Ford, Dearborn, Michigan;

Andrew W. Mellon, Woodland Road, Pittsburgh, Pa.;

Edward T. Stotesbury, Chestnut Hill, Pa.;

George F. Baker, 75 East 93d Street, New
York City;

Winthrop W. Aldrich, Roslyn, Long Island,
New York;

Pierre S. du Pont, Wilmington, Delaware;

Bernard M. Baruch, 120 Broadway, New York City;

Sosthenes Behn, 67 Broad Street, New York City;

Morris L. Clothier, Villa Nova, Pa.;

George W. Childs Drexel, Bryn Mawr, Pennsylvania;

Edward F. Hutton, 2 East 92d Street, New York City;

Vincent Astor, Rhinebeck, New York;

Marshall Field III, 435 East 52d Street, New York City;

Lawrence P. Fisher, Grayhaven, Detroit, Michigan;

Max C. Fleischmann, 595 Madison Avenue, New York City;

Walter E. Frew, 1035 Fifth Avenue, New York City;

Eugene G. Grace, Bethlehem, Pa.;

Edward S. Harkness, 1 East 75th Street, New York City;

Charles Hayden, Savoy-Plaza Hotel, New York City;

Clarence H. Mackay, Roslyn, Long Island, New York;

H. E. Manville, Pleasantville, New York;

[76]

Charles E. Mitchell, 934 Fifth Avenue, New York City;

John J. Raskob, Centreville, Maryland;

Samuel W. Rayburn, 969 Park Avenue, New York City;

Alfred P. Sloan, Jr., 820 Fifth Avenue, New York;

Charles M. Schwab, 21 Riverside Drive, New York;

Gerald Swope, 1040 Park Avenue, New York City;

Edward R. Stettinius, 1030 Fifth Avenue, New York;

Walter C. Teagle, East Port Chester, Conn.;

Albert H. Wiggin, 660 Park Avenue, New York City;

Clarence M. Woolley, 40 West Fortieth Street, New York;

Owen D. Young, 830 Park Avenue, New York City.

Later that day I received another letter:

JOHN DAVISON ROCKEFELLER

January 26, 1937

My dear Mr. President:

I have lived a full and rich life, and soon shall be gathered to my ancestors, where the material things of life will no longer interest me.

I should like to depart this life secure in the knowledge of a final contribution to the welfare and happiness of the American people. In the recent election they have placed their endorsement upon your platform for the redistribution of wealth by electing you President of the United States. I shall accept their collective judgment, since the American people awarded me in my lifetime a fair share of the fruits of labor.

I note that Congress has initiated legislation looking toward the seizure of all wealth in excess of five million dollars for each family. If it will not embarrass your plan, my dear Mr. President, I should like to anticipate the reduction of my own share of worldly goods to the limit decreed by the American people in the last election.

I am therefore disposing in orderly process my possessions in excess of five million dollars. I am making some gifts to persons associated with me during my long span of life. The residue I have instructed my attorneys to turn over to the United States Treasury as a gift to the federal government.

I am reminded that there are precedents for this action. You will recall, my dear Mr. President, that the late Oliver Wendell

Holmes left the residue of his estate to the federal government. In his will he said, in effect:

I have had the use of this money all my life. I cannot take it with me. I do not want to leave my descendants so much that they will become idle parasites, preying on society. I therefore leave it to the government, whose beneficences enabled me to amass it.

In this sentiment I concur. I trust, my dear Mr. President, the government will permit me to redistribute my wealth in this fashion.

With best wishes, my dear Mr. President,

JOHN D. ROCKEFELLER, SR.

A few days later, just as dusk was falling over the city of Washington, my secretary informed me that Mr. Winthrop W. Aldrich, the New York banker, was waiting for me in the White House. He had entered the White House from the east wing, in order to avoid newspapermen. I had my secretary bring him to my office through the building. He was accompanied by his attorney, Mr. William D. Embree.

When he entered my office I recognized him, since I had met him in the Chase National Bank before I became President. We shook hands.

"Sit down, Mr. Aldrich," I said, "What can I do for you?"

"I received your letter."

"I hope you liked it."

"Perhaps I am compelled to like it," Mr. Aldrich replied. "I came here, Mr. President, in behalf of a number of gentlemen who received your recent letter concerning your Share Our Wealth program. A number of us, in response to your invitation, have assembled here in Washington, and we should like to confer with you as soon as possible. We have kept our coming from the press, as you advised us in your letter."

"How soon can you assemble here?" I inquired.

"Within the hour," replied Aldrich.

Aldrich made several telephone calls. I gave my secretary instructions to see that the visitors were escorted to the library in the White House proper. I then left the executive office with Aldrich. On our way through the building I asked him how his markets were holding up in New York.

"The markets remain about the same, Mr. President," he replied, "but there is very little buying and selling. Everybody is waiting to find out just how you intend to seize wealth."

In a very few minutes the visitors began arriv-

"ALL RIGHT HUEY." SAID REED

ing. The first to arrive were Thomas W. Lamont and George Whitney, two partners in the firm of J. P. Morgan & Co., who explained they came to represent J. Pierpont Morgan in the conference. They were accompanied by the Morgan attorney, John W. Davis, one-time Democratic nominee for the Presidency. I had met Mr. Lamont and Mr. Davis previously.

Then came Andrew W. Mellon, accompanied by his son, Paul Mellon, and by his attorney, David A. Reed, the former United States Senator, whom I knew well by reason of his service in the Senate. Then Pierre S. du Pont and Irenée du Pont, accompanied by their attorney, William J. Donovan, the former Assistant Attorney General. Owen D. Young, Charles M. Schwab, and Eugene G. Grace came in next, followed by Bernard M. Baruch. E. T. Stotesbury, the Philadelphia banker and Morgan partner, was the last to arrive.

After all were seated, I asked:

"Is anyone representing Mr. Rockefeller, Jr?"

Mr. Aldrich replied:

"He intends to see you later, Mr. President. He could not join us today."

I surmised that the younger Rockefeller had been badly shaken by his father's action in deeding the bulk of his fortune to the government in compliance with the Share Our Wealth program. I wondered how many more of this crowd knew of the elder Rockefeller's deed; there had been no publicity and I had not given out his letter for publication.

"Is anyone here representing Mr. Ford?" I inquired.

Whitney replied:

"No, Mr. President, we did not consult with him."

Turning to Senator David A. Reed, the Mellon lawyer, I said:

"Now, Dave, I was minded to chase you lawyers out of the room, because it is very difficult for lawyers to reach an agreement. I know that, being a lawyer myself. Now, I don't mind your remaining and listening to the conference, but I don't want you lawyers asking any questions or answering any. I want the men here with the money to do the talking for themselves."

"All right, Huey," said Reed.

"Well, now, gentlemen," I inquired, "what is your pleasure?"

They looked at each other, and Baruch repeated, "Pleasure? That's a good one!"

"Well, then, what are your suggestions for putting the Share Our Wealth program into effect with the least disturbance to commerce, business and industry?" I inquired.

There was no response.

"Well, let me call the roll," I next said. "What do you say, Mr. Mellon?"

I was surprised at the strength of the Pittsburgh financier's voice.

"The sooner we know your plan, I suppose, the better we will be able to discuss it."

"What do you say, Mr. Aldrich?"

"I presumed that you would explain your plan and then we would discuss it at a conference between ourselves, and later present you our views."

"Am I to understand, gentlemen, that there is no mentality in this aggregation wise enough to propose a definite plan for the seizure of great wealth and its redistribution to the masses of our people?" I demanded. "If that is true, and God forbid it, it would only go to prove that the public was being cheated when men of such inferior intelligence amassed so much wealth."

Mr. Stotesbury responded:

"Mr. President, speaking for the gentlemen to whom you sent letters in Philadelphia, I believe your limit of five million dollars is entirely too low to encourage a proper development of private commerce and private industry. I met with a number of gentlemen in Philadelphia, and we agreed that if the limit were extended to twenty-five million dollars, we could join with you in working out a program."

"Mr. President," said Aldrich, attracting my attention, "I don't agree with my good friend from Philadelphia."

I realized instantly that Aldrich knew of the elder Rockefeller's letter to me.

"I feel we must resign ourselves to the five million dollar limit, if your plan is held constitutional by the courts," Aldrich continued. "I came to hear your plan and discuss your method of procedure, if you are ready to give us the details."

"Do I understand, Mr. Aldrich, that you are reconciled to the limitation of your personal fortune to five million dollars?"

"Certainly, Mr. President, if it is constitutional," replied Mr. Aldrich.

"I believe you said you were acting in behalf of John D. Rockefeller, Jr.," I said.

Aldrich nodded.

"What is his position in this matter?" I asked.

"He believes the seizure of private capital through a capital levy is unconstitutional, and that it should be tested in the courts before it is imposed. If it is constitutional, then, of course, there can be no objection by private citizens, since it will become the law of the land. But in either event, he wishes to have the act so drawn that if it is held constitutional, its enforcement will neither disrupt nor destroy American business. For that reason he is perfectly willing to join in perfecting your program."

"How many of you gentlemen share the opinion of Mr. Rockefeller, as expressed by Mr. Aldrich, that the banking, business and industrial leaders of our country should cooperate with me now in the drafting of a program to redistribute your fortunes, whether or not the law ultimately is held constitutional?" I inquired.

Mellon, the two du Ponts, Owen Young, Schwab, and Baruch, nodded their heads in agreement.

"What about the attitude of the Morgan firm on that?" I inquired of Lamont, who had sat silent.

"I could not say, without conferring with Mr. Morgan," replied Lamont. "My understanding with other members of my firm was that I should present our views opposing your plan, and learn its details so I could communicate them to our people."

"Do you share the same views, Mr. Stotesbury?" I asked the Philadelphia capitalist and Morgan banker.

"Mr. President, very frankly, I should like to join in any negotiations for carrying out the Share Our Wealth program in an orderly manner, but, of course, as a lifelong associate of Mr. Morgan, I feel I should be guided by his judgment."

"Well, that seems to leave the Morgan firm out of it," I said.

Turning to Aldrich, I inquired:

"Do you believe Mr. Rockefeller would accept the chairmanship of a committee of business men, bankers and industrialists to draft me a plan to carry out my Share Our Wealth program?"

"I believe so, Mr. President," replied Aldrich, "But I should like to confirm that by telephone."

I indicated the telephone on my desk.

"Call him now," I said.

In a few minutes Aldrich was relating our conversation to John D. Rockefeller, Jr., at his home in New York City. From his replies it was obvious that Mr. Rockefeller was accepting the chairmanship. When Aldrich hung up the phone, he turned around and said:

"Mr. President, Mr. Rockefeller will serve as chairman of your committee."

"That's fine," I said. "His services will allay fear throughout the business world."

I stood up, and my visitors arose in a body.

"Now, Mr. Lamont, Mr. Whitney, Mr. Davis, and Mr. Stotesbury, I believe we can excuse you," I said. "Since you feel that your firm does not care to participate in these conferences, I will abide by your decision."

John W. Davis, the Morgan lawyer, interrupted me.

"Mr. President, if you will forgive me, may I say a word?" he inquired.

I nodded.

"Mr. President, I think Mr. Lamont should be given permission to return to the conference after consulting with the other members of the firm," he said. "I feel sure that when the developments of this conference are reported to Mr. Morgan, he will desire to participate along with the other gentlemen."

"I am sorry, Mr. Davis, but your client, Mr. Morgan is refusing to accept the Share Our Wealth program," I replied. "Acting apparently upon your advice, he is going to fight it in the courts. Now, I am perfectly willing to follow the Constitution and to accept his challenge and battle it out in the courts. Recognizing him as an enemy of the Share Our Wealth Program, I don't feel it is proper to have him or any of his agents participate in any way in the drafting of the program.

"Without reflecting upon the honor or integrity of Mr. Morgan or his associates, it would be difficult to convince the American people that their active cooperation in the drafting of the plan would be for any other purpose than to weaken it or to write some loophole into it through which they might escape or defeat it in the courts. Now, I believe these other gentlemen are cooperating in good faith and will draft a plan to the best of their ability.

"In the final analysis, of course, I shall rely on them for the economic sections of the bill, but I will be forced to rely upon my own attorney general and solicitor general for the constitutional sections in the event there is any difference of opinion between this committee and the government's legal advisors."

Davis bowed. With Lamont, Whitney, and Stotesbury, he left the room.

After they departed, I said to those remaining:

"Now, gentlemen, I appoint John D. Rockefeller, Jr. chairman of a National Share Our Wealth Committee, and I appoint as additional members Andrew W. Mellon, Winthrop W. Aldrich, Pierre S. du Pont, Irenée du Pont, Owen D. Young, Charles M. Schwab, and Bernard M.

Baruch. I further empower Mr. Rockefeller as chairman to name such additional members as he may desire, upon sole condition that he shall name no member from the firm of J. P. Morgan or its Philadelphia ally, Drexel and Company. You, Mr. Aldrich, will communicate that authority to Mr. Rockefeller.

"Now, gentlemen, will you join me at dinner?" They did. To my surprise, it turned out to be a friendly dinner. Mr. Pierre du Pont rather startled his associates by saying he was heartily in favor of the Share Our Wealth program. He said he felt that five million dollars was a trifle low for a limit on a fortune, because some individuals, by their genius, might create a business, as had he and his brother and cousins, the value of which might be increased by wise management from a few million dollars to hundreds of millions of dollars. He expressed fear that future government seizure of fortunes in excess of five million dollars a year would disrupt the operation of an industry.

I was surprised, too, by the views of old Andy Mellon. He told us that his fortune had become a tremendous bother and nuisance. It was apparent to me that he was an unhappy man, and that he wanted above all to have the affection of the American people, which he believed he had lost

[89]

through no fault of his own. He appeared willing to assume a role in the Share Our Wealth program. Before the dinner ended, I named him Vice-Chairman of the Committee, and his face lighted with real pleasure when I made the appointment.

After dinner I said:

"Now, gentlemen, you will be called together, I presume, by Mr. Rockefeller, and undoubtedly you will meet in New York City. When you are ready, bring your plan to me."

V

Wherein the Masters of Finance are Ours

With Morgan balking, John D. Rockefeller, Jr. heads committee to redistribute wealth and his committee of multi-millionaires devises Share Our Wealth Corporation; a report is completed; Congress is addressed by the new President; the redistribution of wealth begins.

"THE National Share Our Wealth Committee is ready to report its plan for decentralizing great wealth, Mr. President."

This statement by my secretary thrilled me. It was made only a fortnight after my appointment of the National Share Our Wealth Committee under the Chairmanship of John D. Rockefeller, Jr.

"That's wonderful news," I exclaimed. "Those multi-millionaires have a patriotic streak in them, after all."

"Mr. Rockefeller's secretary just telephoned me, seeking an appointment," my secretary informed me. "He can be down here tonight."

"Fine," I said. "Any time he arrives, have him come in by the east entrance again. Tell him to bring along as many members of the committee as he wishes."

Mr. John D. Rockefeller, Jr., Mr. Andrew W. Mellon, Mr. Owen D. Young, Mr. Charles M. Schwab, Mr. Bernard Baruch, and Mr. Winthrop W. Aldrich arrived at the White House about nine-thirty that night. After exchanging greetings, Mr. Rockefeller said:

"I am privileged, Mr. President, to report that your National Share Our Wealth Committee has decided on a plan for the redistribution of wealth. Our committee was unanimous in its conclusions. We have prepared a report recommending the enactment of this particular plan, if you persist in your present intention to have Congress impose a capital levy, seizing all fortunes in excess of five million dollars. We do not render any findings upon the constitutionality of either the capital levy or the operation of this plan. Our lawyers have prepared a separate brief demonstrating the constitutionality of this plan of redistribution of wealth. It is with real pleasure, Mr. President, that I now hand you our complete report."

With these words Mr. Rockefeller handed me a leather-bound volume the gold-tinted inscription on the outside cover of which read:

REPORT

of

THE NATIONAL SHARE OUR WEALTH COMMITTEE

to the

PRESIDENT OF THE UNITED STATES
February 15, 1937.

"First, let me congratulate you, Mr. Rockefeller, on the great patriotic service rendered the

American people by your committee in so prompt-
ly preparing this report," I told him. "Let me
thank you and your associates in their name."

As I spoke, I leafed through the voluminous report. I noticed that there was almost a score of
names signed to it. I noted Rockefeller and Mellon headed the signers. I noted the names of
Albert G. Milbank, Frank L. Polk and William
D. Embree were among those signed. I observed,
too, that the brief of which Mr. Rockefeller had
spoken also was printed in this volume. In the
rear of the volume was the copy of a bill.

Mr. Rockefeller was watching me as I leafed
through this book. As I reached the portion containing the bill, he said:

"Mr. President, our lawyers have drafted that
bill, which embodies our plan. We have recommended its enactment."

"That's splendid, Mr. Rockefeller," I said. "But
now won't you tell briefly just what your plan
does?"

"Certainly, Mr. President," replied the oil king.
"First we propose the creation of a federal organization to be incorporated under the name of the
Federal Share Our Wealth Corporation. We propose that it shall operate as a steward and trustee
for the American people in the redistribution of

wealth. It shall have the power only of a manager and agent for the people.

"We propose that the government, in seizing wealth, shall leave management of every industry or business in the hands of those people now controlling it, until matters get better arranged. We propose that the surplus of wealth in every family owning more than five million dollars shall be converted into the form of securities, which in turn shall be turned over to this corporation to hold in trust for the American people. This corporation shall then issue its own stock, which can then be distributed among the peoples according to any plan deemed suitable by Congress.

"The national survey of wealth and of the requirements of our people to live in comfort, ordered by Congress, will soon be initiated. When it is completed, Congress itself will receive the report on the wealth to be seized and the requirements to be provided. The committee has dealt solely with the problem of seizing the wealth."

"Now, let me follow you, Mr. Rockefeller," I interrupted him. "First, you propose that surplus wealth shall be turned into the form of securities; then you propose that those securities shall be turned over to this federal corporation to be held in trust for the benefit of the American people,

"MR. PRESIDENT . . . . . . THE REPORT."

and, third, you propose that this corporation itself shall issue stock which may be distributed among the people."

"That's correct, Mr. President," said Rockefeller.

"Now, you mentioned a moment ago that the management of private business and private industry will be left in the hands of those now controlling it," I continued. "How do you do that?"

"Let me give you a definite illustration: Let us take the firm of J. P. Morgan and Company. It is a limited partnership. Let us say that the government has levied a capital tax of $175,000,000 on the partnership in that firm, and suppose that the assets of J. P. Morgan and Company are valued at $200,000,000. This would mean that the capital levy on the Morgan partnership would take away $175,000,000 of its assets, and leave the partners with only $25,000,000 of the assets.

"Now, we propose to authorize the partners to issue two types of stock, both bearing equal dividends. One form of stock would have voting powers. The other would have no such powers for the time being. The Morgan partners would issue $25,000,000 of voting stock to themselves. They would turn over $175,000,000 of the non-voting stock to the Federal Share Our Wealth Corporation. In this manner the assets of the corporation would be seized, but the management of it would temporarily remain with Mr. Morgan and his partners."

"Maybe that is all right," I said. "Now, if I understand you correctly, the corporation would hold all the private stock in trust for the American people, and issue its own stock for redistribution to the people who lack their fair share of American wealth. Why do you have this corporation issue its own stock? Why doesn't it distribute the stock that is seized?"

"To protect the individual, Mr. President, against fluctuations in the earning power of different corporations in different years. Let me illustrate. If you and I are both poor men, we each are awarded ten shares of $100 par value stock—say I am given Sears-Roebuck stock and you receive Pennsylvania Railroad stock. In the year in which we are awarded this stock, both companies are paying 5 per cent dividends. We each receive in the first year $50 in income from the stock. In the second year, two great Sears-Roebuck factories are destroyed by fire, at a terrific loss to the corporation. On the other hand, the Pennsylvania notes a 30 per cent increase in its traffic, with a consequent heavy increase in its revenue and profits for the year. The results are that the value of my Sears-Roebuck stock has been reduced from $1,000 to $750, and it pays no dividend at all that year. On the other hand, the value of your Pennsylvania stock has risen to $1,250, and the dividend is up to 6 per cent, and you receive $60 in dividends. I have a capital loss and no income from my stock. You have a capital accretion and an increase in dividend.

"Now, by giving the Federal Share Our Wealth Corporation power to issue its own stock, it would hold both my original $1,000 of Sears-Roebuck and your original $1,000 of Pennsylvania Railroad Stock. You and I both receive $1,000 of Federal Share Our Wealth Corporation stock, paying 5 per cent or $50 in dividends. Now, the Sears-Roebuck fires and its capital losses would have but little effect upon the total dividends received by the Federal Share Our Wealth Corporation, but admit there was some decrement in the corporation's revenues. It might reduce its dividend from 5 to $4\frac{1}{2}$ per cent, or 4 per cent, in which case the value of the $1,000 stock I received would be unaffected, as would yours, while each of us would receive either $45 or $40 in dividends the second year. We recommended that plan, Mr. President, solely for the protection of the people who are to

38113

benefit from the redistribution of wealth."

"I understand it now," I said. "But how would we protect the interests of the American people in the Morgan firm? Suppose, Mr. Rockefeller, that in order to defeat our plan, Mr. Morgan's partners, having lost $175,000,000 of their wealth, would deliberately mismanage the business of that firm? Having lost $175,000,000 it might be possible that they wouldn't care what happened to their remaining $25,000,000, if they could succeed in destroying the value of the $175,000,000 redistributed among the American people. How could we protect the interest of those people in that firm?"

"Easily, Mr. President. The Federal Share Our Wealth Corporation is a steward and trustee of that stock," replied Rockefeller. "As a good steward, and under its duty as a trustee, that corporation would quickly note any mismanagement of the Morgan firm, and would be empowered to enter the nearest Federal court, produce its stock, make its charge of mismanagement, and ask for the appointment of a receiver. The same procedure would be followed as is followed now by minority stockholders or creditors who seek receiverships in order to protect their investments or credits. There is nothing novel in the procedure. Our attorneys have covered this subject fully in their brief."

"You have studied your plan," I said. "I presume it applies as well to non-incorporated industrial or commercial holdings and to corporate holdings, as well as it does to partnerships."

"Oh, yes, Mr. President. In the case of some corporations, as the attorneys have pointed out in the brief, it may be necessary to slightly modify a few of the state corporation laws to permit the issuance of non-voting stocks. But I am sure we will have the immediate cooperation of the states in that minor respect."

"Are you gentlemen willing to defend this plan before Congress?" I asked.

"We would be very glad to, Mr. President, if that will be of any help to you," replied Rockefeller.

"Now, gentlemen, I have one more request," I said. "On your return to New York, I should like you to make this plan public. I shall issue a statement, after consulting with the Attorney General and the Solicitor General, once your plan has gone to the country. As I said when I appointed you, I shall rely on my Attorney General and my Solicitor General for advice on all constitutional points. Aside from that, I am willing to accord great respect to your views on economic phases of the Share Our Wealth Program. You have said there is nothing in your plan in violation of the Constitution. I have had my own plan for the last four years. It differs considerably from this, in some respects, and my own plan includes the redistribution of the wealth. I am satisfied that taking your plan for seizing the wealth and adding to it my own method for redistributing it, we will have a perfectly effective program for sharing our wealth. I want to commend you gentlemen again, and I shall not hesitate to do so publicly after you have announced your plan to the American people. Your assistance has been a very valuable contribution to the restoration of prosperity and the assurance of life, liberty and the pursuit of happiness to our fellow citizens, who have been denied these constitutional guaranties by poverty in the past."

The next afternoon's newspapers in screaming editorial headlines carried the news to a waiting populace that the barons of Wall Street were content at last to accept democracy in America. Having conferred all morning with my Attorney General and Solicitor General, and finding they concurred in the conclusions of the committee's attorneys that the Rockefeller Committee's plan was constitutional, I issued a statement from the White House approving its general outline, subject to some modifications on management and for a more effective distribution later. I praised the splendid cooperation of the committee's personnel in the Share Our Wealth program.

Some little while later Henry Ford and his son, Edsel, were announced in the old Lincoln study on the second floor of the White House. I exchanged the usual greetings with them.

"Mr. President," said Henry Ford, getting down to business at once, "my son and I came here tonight to tell you in person that we are accepting your Share Our Wealth program without reservation and without condition. We have been preparing for it ever since your election. Now, we have a plan by which we will share our own wealth. We bring it to you tonight for your approval. If it will interfere with the government's plan for redistributing wealth, we will abandon it, and abide by whatever arrangement the government sees fit to impose upon us."

"What is your plan, Mr. Ford?" I inquired.

"Mr. President, as you know, I have built up a vast organization, reaching into every state of the Union. Aside from my automobile factories around Detroit, we have assembling plants in scores of cities. We have agencies everywhere. We have ore mines, steel mills, glass works, and a vast

[103]

assortment of other interests. It is a tremendous organization, and we were a little fearful that the government's redistribution of our wealth would disrupt and destroy that organization. We hope that the government will permit us to redistribute our own wealth so that we may keep this organization intact."

"How great is your wealth, Mr. Ford?"

"Mr. President, I cannot estimate it," replied Ford. "I actually mean that. It includes so many properties on which we have placed an arbitrary value. For instance, we construct a glass factory with materials manufactured in our own plants, using our own workmen. Its cost to us is $400,000. We figure it out that if we use the same machinery and the same man power in manufacturing automobiles, we would produce cars which would give us a profit of $300,000. Therefore, we place an arbitrary value on that glass plant of $700,000. On the other hand, if a private contractor had built the plant, he would have charged us one million dollars. In prosperous times, the plant could be capitalized and sold for a million and a half, or two million dollars. During this depression, a private owner might have been glad to get rid of it for $500,000 and probably couldn't find a buyer at that price. Based upon the return on capital, the plant might be valued at $100,000, its junking value, because we perhaps have not turned a wheel in it in the last eight months. Now we face the same tortuous process in fixing values on hundreds of our properties. So you see, Mr. President, it is almost impossible for us to place a definite estimate on our wealth, because so much of it is represented by physical property. We may be worth $200,000,000 under some conditions, and our properties may be worth a billion dollars under others."

"Well, what is your plan, Mr. Ford?"

"Both my son Edsel and I are content with the five million dollar limit. We want to keep that share of our properties. Now, we plan to retain control of our properties by dividing their ownership among long-term Ford employees. We propose to use the money invested outside the Ford organization to construct homes for loyal Ford employees not now owning their own homes. That will be a free gift to the Ford employees. We will build different homes for different types of employees, but we will provide at least a $5,000 home for those not now owning homes. We own land now in the Detroit area, and we can build these homes at nominal cost by using our own materials and our own organization.

"We propose, further, to issue stock against the physical value of our properties, placing a fair capitalization—as fair as our economists can fix it—on each property, and issue stock against it. Then we propose to divide that stock among our workers. We believe that the loyalty of Ford workers will keep the Ford family in control of the Ford Company for generations to come. Now, there may be some surplus left when we have finished the distribution of our wealth under this plan. The surplus would be turned over to the government."

"Splendid, Mr. Ford, splendid," I said. "I hope every rich man will follow your wonderful example. But, bear in mind you will have to do all this before Congress passes the Share Our Wealth law, with its capital levy. Once that goes into effect, I doubt whether you could carry out your plan."

"How soon will that law be enacted, Mr. President?"

"Not for another thirty days," I replied.

"Oh, that will give us plenty of time," replied Ford. "Now, Mr. President, one thing more. Will you permit us to make the announcement of our plan in our own way, and when we deem it advisable?"

"Why, certainly, Mr. Ford. I'm so happy to

have you cooperate with me that I shall place no obstacle in your path."

The Fords departed. I secretly longed to reveal their plan instantly to the public, because I knew it would set a splendid example to other men of bloated wealth; but I was content to let the Fords carry out their own plan in their own way.

A messenger from the House of Representatives brought a note to the White House requesting that I appear before that body and explain in detail certain questions relative to the Share Our Wealth legislation which I would propose. I responded by announcing that I welcomed the opportunity to address the House at four o'clock on the same afternoon, urging that members of the United States Senate be invited to be present. Contained in my official note of acceptance to make the address before the House of Representatives was the following:

I would ask that the House vary its customary rule so that all members of Congress, both of the House and the Senate, who desire to do so, may propound whatever questions they may wish. I would prefer, of course, as far as possible, these questions be submitted in writing.

At four o'clock in the afternoon, when I arrived to begin my address to the members of Congress, I hurriedly reviewed the questions which had been submitted to me in writing. There were probably twenty written questions. I soon saw that with the exception of three of them, my general address would answer the inquiries.

I spoke at some length—for a period of nearly three hours. In the course of my address I said:

> We do not propose any division of property. We propose that no one man shall own too much, and that no one family shall have too little for comfort. There is a sane limit to the amount of water that a horse can drink; to the number of miles than a man can run; to the length of time which one can live. There is also a sane limit to the amount of wealth which it is healthy for one to own.
>
> It may be that the proportions which I suggest are too high or too low, but for the present I ask the law-makers to provide that when a man gets enough wealth so that he has one hundred times as much as the average family in the country, then we say he has reached his limit. Our average wealth at normal values amounts to about $17,000 to each family. So we would say that when one possesses wealth amounting to $1,700,-000, he has enough, and that for him to have more than that sum would mean that he

has more business to handle than his two eyes
and ears can safely manage, but, worse than
that, he can have that much only by taking
away from his neighbors something they need
for comfort.

"Now, we propose that likewise we must
not force a family to survive on too little.
How much is too little? For the present we
have proposed that no family should ever
have less than the substantial home comforts
of a value equal to one-third of the average
family wealth. That is to say, the mother
and children of every breadwinner have the
right under our laws to expect not to fall further than two-thirds the distance below the
average family wealth. In dollars and cents,
at normal values based on our accepted average family wealth of $17,000, there would be
no family in this country which would possess
less than the reasonable home comforts and
conveniences of a value of from $5,000 to
$6,000, free of debt.

Now someone may say that the energy,
ability and genius of a man whose fortune is
limited to less than two million dollars are no
longer alive unless he is permitted to accumulate more. Admitting that to be true, though
I do not believe it, nevertheless it is better for
this nation that it give hope and encourage-
ment to the ambitions and aspirations of

125,000,000 more people rather than to excite the greed of fifty-eight. There are probably several millions of people whose genius will prove equal, if not superior, to the good that is to be found in the greed of fifty-eight.

There are, however, men in the Congress of the United States who have sacrificed fortunes to serve the people. In the yellow fever epidemics there were men who gave their lives for the cause of science. If America for its greatness must depend on exciting supergreed for the sake of modern and greater development, then we have set a bad example to the great inventors, to our great scientists, and to those of us here who manage the country for a mere living.

And now it is further necessary that I say the time may come when we should declare that a guarantee of one-third of the average is not sufficient for our country's better development. If that time should come, it may be necessary to lower the amount which the big man would be allowed to own. It might so happen that in the future the limit of $1,700,000 to each fortune would be reduced to $1,000,000 or even less than that. For instance, we may have so many more people worth a million dollars or worth a half-million dollars than we have now, because money will be so much easier to make, that we will have to lower our limit. Whatever that limit may be, we will never allow our people to be deprived of the substantial comforts of life.

Now we will further propose that the earnings of no family shall be less than one-third the earnings of the average family, which means that no family income shall be less than $2,500 per year, based upon what the best experts of our country estimate if all are allowed to produce. In order to accomplish this we must establish a limit to the amount of earnings which a big man may have. In that particular, we would say to begin with that no one should earn more than one hundred times the average family income, which would mean not more than $750,000 per year in earnings to any one man.

Something must be done about our debt structure and the burden of taxation. Our debts today, both public and private, amount to $262,000,000,000. Figured at an average interest rate of 6%, the interest charges alone on this debt each year amount to $15,-720,000,000. To this, if you will add the cost of taxation, each year the interest and taxes demand of the national income more than two-thirds of what has been made during the hard times. Something must be done to reduce the debt structure.

Wherever the Bible decrees a policy, undertaking to defy such a mandate of the Scriptures has never led to other than ruin for any nation. In endeavoring to carry this debt structure on the backs of the masses, this country invites certain ruin.

We will propose an actual old age pension adequate and sufficient to care for those who should be retired from the ranks of labor, without one having to take the pauper's oath, as the so-called Roosevelt legislation requires. Where the income of any person does not exceed $1,000 a year or where the possessions of such persons do not amount to a value of $5,000 they will be entitled to draw the old age allowance.

Care and attention will be given for the debts which we owe to our soldiers; for the education and training of the youth of this land; for national defense; but above all things, for the general upbuilding and preservation of the country, and for avoiding any foreign entanglements of any kind or nature."

As I was about to conclude, one member arose and asked:

"Would the President permit a question from the floor?"

"Certainly," I answered.

"My question is this: Since you limit the

"I CANNOT ESTIMATE MY WEALTH"

amount which one may own to $5,000,000 to start with, by this tax being collected every year fortunes will be reduced to approximately $1,700,-000 to the person in a few years. How will there be any more big businesses; will this mean that all big businesses will have to be divided up, brick by brick?"

"No," I answered. "I thoroughly explained that point preceding the election, but I will take the time to explain it to you again. It is the same as it would be if a man died and left his property to be divided among his heirs. In this case, it so happens that many of the American people become the heirs instead of a few sons and daughters. We do not propose to break up big enterprises. All that we will do will be to provide that more people will share in the profits and ownership of big enterprises. In other words, instead of one man drawing down several million dollars out of the earnings in a year, the company will make just as much money as ever, but there will be thousands, maybe hundreds of thousand, perhaps millions of people drawing what formerly a few people drew in the way of profits. We do not care how big the business grows so long as it is efficient for the country. Our concern is that their ownership should not be concentrated in too few people, and that their profits should be shared by the people more widely."

A United States Senator arose and said:

"It seems that many of us will have to exercise a great deal of faith and hope."

"Yes, brother," I answered, "and in that connection it would not hurt if some of you would read the 13th Chapter, I Corinthians." *

* I. Corinthians, Chapter 13:
Though I speak with the tongues of men and of angels, and have not charity, I am become as sounding brass, or a tinkling cymbal.

And though I have the gift of prophecy, and understand all mysteries, and all knowledge; and though I have all faith, so that I could remove mountains, and have not charity, I am nothing.

And though I bestow all my goods to feed the poor, and though I give my body to be burned, and have not charity, it profiteth me nothing.

Charity suffereth long, and is kind; charity envieth not; charity vaunteth not itself, is not puffed up,

Doth not behave itself unseemly, seeketh not her own, is not easily provoked, thinketh no evil;

Rejoiceth not in iniquity, but rejoiceth in the truth;

Beareth all things, believeth all things, hopeth all things, endureth all things.

Charity never faileth: but whether there be prophecies, they shall fail; whether there be tongues, they shall cease; whether there be knowledge, it shall vanish away.

For we know in part, and we prophecy in part.

But when that which is perfect is come, then that which is in part shall be done away.

When I was a child, I spake as a child, I understood as a child, I thought as a child: but when I became a man, I put away childish things.

For now we see through a glass, darkly; but then face to face: now I know in part; but then shall I know even as also I am known.

And now abideth faith, hope, charity, these three; but the greatest of these is charity.

[114]

The laws* which Congress enacted not only re-distributed wealth and income among the people, but the same laws also levied the taxes for the future support of the government in such a way that the wealth of the country would never again accumulate in a few hands. They likewise made simple and ample provision to insure the man at the bottom from ever owning less than the home and comforts of life which he was originally guaranteed, free of any debt.

Thus I had taken the first step to provide every man, woman and child with the proper food, clothing and shelter—as I had promised them in the campaign.

* See Appendix for substance of laws mentioned.

VI

Wherein Rebellion Brews and Fades

A Governor threatens uprising; the people's resentment; the President comes to the Governor's aid; the appeal to the court; the Supreme Court decides on Share Our Wealth; a member of the Bar attends court.

WHEN the Congress had adjourned after passing the Share Our Wealth legislation, I immediately signed the bills and announced that they were the law of the land. The basis underlying most of the legislation was a perfect model to prevent future accumulations of property in the hands of a small number of people to such an extent as would impose consequent poverty upon the masses.

Five die-hard Senators staged a filibuster against the capital levy tax bill, which, while lasting less than two days, aroused such public sentiment as to leave it beyond doubt that the American people not only approved, but in whole heart expected and demanded the enactment of the Share Our Wealth legislation in toto.

I decided to spend a few days away from the Capitol at a hunting and fishing lodge belonging to some of my friends. I had made all arrangements to depart, and intended to leave at an early hour of the evening. Suddenly the door of my private office opened and my secretary rushed in, holding in his hand a news agency dispatch.

"The Governor of the State of———————— has announced today that his state would resist by force, if necessary, any attempt to enforce the national Share Our Wealth legislation," said my secretary hurriedly.

"Let me have that paper," I said. "Let's see what he is saying."

I took the paper from my secretary's hands and read from it the following:

> The Governor of —————— today called for the nearby New England states to join in a concerted resistance to the Share Our Wealth legislation enacted in Congress. The Governor declared that he was prepared to resist any effort which might be made to limit the size of fortunes honestly accumulated within the confines of the Commonwealth. He considers that all guarantees of the national republic are swept aside by legislation which would immediately result in the confiscation of fortunes in excess of five million dollars which will gradually be forced down to $1,700,000 to any one person. The Governor's statement follows:

I read no further. I turned to my secretary.

"We will just change our plans for the weekend. Make our destination the capital of this Governor's state. Arrange for an aeroplane. There will be about ten people in our party."

"When do you wish to leave?"

"At about the time we had prepared to leave.

If it is at all possible, let's get away without it being known that we are leaving, or, at all events, where we are going."

"But Mr. President," my secretary asked, "should you not have a little more protection than the few men you are taking, under the circumstances?"

"It is not I who need protection—it is the Governor. He is going to need protection, and I think I should get there soon. I doubt that there is anyone but I who can protect him. I had always thought the man had better sense. He has been in office only a few weeks."

I called the two U. S. Senators from that state. I pledged them to the utmost secrecy, and after a short conference arranged that they would accompany me to ————————. Shortly after 10 o'clock a party of nine, including myself, left the Washington airport headed for ————————, the capital of the state. We were sure that not more than a half-dozen people had seen us depart, and precautions had been taken to insure that they would not divulge the information.

The ride to ———————— was very pleasant and without event. I discussed at some length with the two Senators the situation brought about by the Governor's hasty announcement.

"My idea," said the senior Senator, "is that our best plan would be to get in touch with the Governor as early as possible. Maybe before morning a satisfactory statement could be issued which would set the matter at rest."

"That is not my idea, Senator," I answered. "This thing is going to break out somewhere, and somebody must beat his breast, and it might just as well be your Governor as another one. I think he will find, by the time we see him, that he is in need of our help, and that we need no help from him."

"I do not understand," answered the Senator.

"Well, Senator, those people in ——————— are just as much in need of this program as anybody else. It is life to 95 per cent of them. If they have the idea that their Governor has suspended or frustrated these bills, which mean their immediate life and comfort, there has never been a mob collected that will equal the one that will be after him."

"Oh, you will never see a mob in my home town," said the junior Senator.

"I won't? Now, I know nothing about your home town and you do, but I know humanity. There will be a mob in ——————— by the time we get there, unless they are vastly different from what I understand human beings to be. But that is a matter which can wait; a few more hours will determine it."

"Maybe you are right," said the senior Senator.

We arrived at ——————— airport shortly after midnight. General Smedley Butler, the Secretary of War, had stationed a score of soldiers, who immediately interned the few persons who were at the airport, so that our arrival should not become known to the public. I spent the night at the private home of a friend of the senior Senator in the suburbs of the capital city. The next morning it was the Senator who awakened me. He laughed nervously as he spoke:

"Huey, I think you know ——————— just as well as you do the rest of the country. Hell's popping. No one can find the Governor."

"Well, I think you and I can find him. The chances are he is still in the capital. He will be glad to see us."

"I don't think so," answered the Senator. "They tell me there were a hundred speeches denouncing him in this town last night."

"Poor fellow!"

"I think you are the only man who can save him. It's a good thing you came."

I reached for the telephone at the side of my

bed. I called the Governor's Mansion. Someone answered. I said to him:

"Now, take my word, this is the President of the United States talking to you. I must talk to the Governor at once. If he is not there I must know where he is."

"Give me your number and I will have the Governor call you, Mr. President—if you are the President. Are you in Washington?"

"No, I am in ——————, right here where the Governor needs me most. I want him to call me here."

"Just a moment," he answered.

I waited a few minutes. Another voice was at the telephone:

"You say this is the President?" it asked.

"Yes, this is the President—Huey P. Long. I think you will recognize from my voice that I am the President."

"Well, hello, Mr. President. This is the Governor. What can I do for you?"

"What can I do for *you?*" I asked.

"Well, where can I see you?"

"I am some distance away. Do you think you can reach me all right if I give you the address?"

"I will try my best," he answered. "Maybe you would like to come here for breakfast."

"Maybe I had better come there, breakfast or no breakfast."

"I wish you would," he answered.

"I'm on my way," I said, and hung up the telephone receiver.

There were about a hundred people scattered about the streets within a block of the Governor's Mansion, somewhat more than I would have expected. We did not have to ring the door bell. The attendant was expecting us and I was recognized by some members of the crowd as I entered the Mansion grounds. I, of course, knew that the secrecy of my whereabouts could be preserved but little longer.

I met the Governor.

"Well, Mr. President," he said to me, "it is always a pleasure to meet the first citizen of the land."

"Yes," I said, "it is, of course, a great honor for me to meet the first citizen of the great Commonwealth of ——————. How is your rebellion?"

As he seated himself, I drew a chair close to the middle-aged new Chief Executive of the state. I leaned close to him and repeated:

"How is your rebellion?"

"All right," he answered, "but you have all the

rebels."

"I thought so," I answered. "What has happened since your announcement of yesterday?"

"I think I was misunderstood somewhat," the Governor spoke slowly. "You see, the people read the headlines rather than my statement. Fortunately, I did not leave the Mansion last night, or I would have had serious trouble. I might not be alive. Down the street here one of my close friends was quite seriously hurt, and two or three others were threatened. Somebody took charge of the Capitol grounds and called a meeting on the south side. I understand they have called a meeting for this morning to be held in the big park across from the Capitol. Of course, that doesn't worry me particularly. We won't have mob rule here."

"Well, now, you know, as the Governor you have the right to call out the militia, and I would say that 999 times out of a thousand the militia will respond just as the Governor orders; but would you like to call out the militia to fight the Share Our Wealth laws and see how those men would respond?"

"No! That is not my idea. My idea is to preserve order."

"I see. Your statement indicated that you were going to prevent the national legislation from applying in this state with the use of the militia. I am afraid you will have to explain to your militia when you call them that your action is to preserve order, and that you don't intend to thwart United States' laws."

"Well, Mr. President, since you are here, it might be you could help me in the matter by explaining that the purpose was for law and order."

"Oh, you want me to handle the matter. Well, I can, quiet them without calling on the militia."

"Very well. All I want, of course, is order preserved."

"Now look here," I said to him, "we might as well talk frankly to one another. I know the bankers elected you Governor of this state, and I know that when you issued that statement yesterday you imagined that you would be the last standard bearer of their idea of government. Now, you see what you have done; you know the consequences, whether you knew them then or not. I am willing to save your face. There are only two courses open to you: one of them is to resign as Governor, which you do not want to do, and I do not want you to have to do; the other is for you to tender your resignation as the agent of the financiers of this country.

"Do you know Mr. Morgan's telephone number?

If you don't, I do,—that is, my office knows it. It seems as if it has been the property of the White House for many years."

"Yes, I know it," he said.

"Then I think you had better tender your resignation to Mr. Morgan, and let him extend the notice to the balance of that small financial clique of the country which attempts to resist this legislation. There are only a few of them left now."

"But isn't there some way that I could relent on the grounds of the acts of the legislation of Congress being upheld by the courts? Wouldn't that be a better way?

"By the way," he continued, "all your laws are going to the courts anyway, sometime."

"You are right," I said.

"Well, following the speech you made in the Senate one day, that the State of Louisiana could file a suit in the Supreme Court, I looked the matter up, and to my surprise found that a state could take that short route to get a quick decision. Why not let us bring that suit, and if you win, then our position is that we are following the law as the court finds it to be."

"Well, now, that's not a bad idea," I stated. "An agreed statement of facts in a suit filed by a state would secure a very early decision of that

"HOW IS THE REBELLION"

law suit. That might be a good idea."

"Then what will I say now?"

"Just say it is a matter for the courts to decide; that in the meantime you will uphold the legislation as the law of the land."

He paused a moment before speaking, then he said:

"I do not know that I want to have it appear that I am the champion fighting the legislation in the courts. My people are for this legislation, it appears, although I was elected on another ticket."

"All right, let's do it this way: let's say that there is to be a friendly test in the Supreme Court. You are to bring the suit for the State of ——— and allow the financial interests the opportunity to file their briefs and to argue the matter, as against those whom we will select to defend the stand of the Government."

"Well, can we issue a statement?"

"Why, sure," I said. "Very glad to do that."

"Well, we will go to the Capitol and write that statement out."

"How about delivering it to the crowd?"

"What crowd?" he said.

"Oh, you have one at the Capitol by now."

"How do you know?"

"From what you have told me. It will be there

waiting for you."

"Then let's go together."

The Governor and I rode into the Capitol grounds and walked up the steps. There was a large crowd. There were some jeers at the Governor, but the general cheering drowned it out. I stopped at the top of the Capitol steps. There I delivered my short speech to the crowd. I said:

> There seems to be some misunderstanding. I desire that the legislation recently passed by Congress shall be tested in the courts by the most simple, direct and expeditious route possible. That course can best be done in a friendly suit, filed by a state directly in the Supreme Court. My friend, the Governor, has agreed to assist us in facilitating an early decision in this matter by filing suit in the name of the State of ——————— in the Supreme Court of the United States on an agreed statement of facts. In that manner there will be an early argument and an early decision, and I am sure that that decision will uphold the validity of the legislation which has been passed. In the meantime, the law of the land will take its usual course, and all of our citizens will begin to share in the benefits. Please do not misunderstand the attitude of either the Governor or myself. If the legislation should not be constitutional, I should

not wish to urge it; if it is constitutional, the Governor will be one of its chief supporters.

I thank you people and the Governor for the opportunity which you are giving in facilitating an early decision by our court of highest resort on the validity of our worth-while legislation.

There was more applause from the crowd. I bowed, and the Governor bowed. We retired to the Executive Offices of the Governor.

"Who took down my speech?" I asked the Governor.

"Our office had it taken," he answered.

"Have it transcribed and let me sign it, so that the newspapers and radio stations will make no mistake."

I stayed only a few more minutes at the Capitol, after which I departed for the airport and headed back to Washington.

* * * *

After the suit filed by the State of ——————— had been argued in the Supreme Court of the United States, I busied myself working out the details for fully carrying out the laws enacted by Congress. We awaited the final decision of the Court on the constitutionality of our laws. The general consensus in the nation, which seemed to

be shared by an almost unanimous sentiment of
the lawyers, was that the legislation would be held
valid and constitutional,—in fact, the members of
the Bar representing the financiers of the country
expected the laws to be upheld.

We were kept very busy setting up the
organization to carry out the general program. I
knew the youth of the country would never understand delay in starting their courses in college.

"Now, here," I said to some of the men in charge
of that detail, "I have said that we will have every
youth in the colleges of professional or vocational
education and training, regardless of the ability of
parents to pay. Every boy and girl is ready and
we must be ready."

"But," responded one, "the teachers are a problem we must consider, too."

"Yes," I replied, "but none of the teachers is
to receive less than from $2,000 to $2,500 for the
year's work. They'll be glad to follow their pro-
fessions now."

In working out the plans to provide for homestead comforts for every family, the state organizations were fast whipping the program into shape
with much less difficulty than we expected.

Our Senate leaders were collaborating with a
number of economists and industrial leaders in

working out hours of labor and the minimum earning for every family. They had reported they felt sure a minimum income of $2,500 per year to every family could be worked out. We preferred a 30 hour week.

We worked at top speed so as to be ready for action immediately following the Supreme Court's decision.

One Saturday afternoon the Chief Justice announced that the Court would deliver its opinion on the Share Our Wealth laws on the following Monday morning, which was one week earlier than the date when most of the decisions were expected to be rendered.

On Monday I had expected to wait at the Executive Offices of the White House for the Court's decision. Somehow I could not quiet a certain restlessness. I was a member of the Bar of the Supreme Court; I had practiced there. In the past, when I was concerned with a decision of that Court, I had attended to hear the judgments read. The thought struck me, why should a difference in positions affect my right as an attorney of that Court to be present at the reading of the decision?

I called for an automobile and rode to the Supreme Court Building. I immediately went to the room where the Court held its sessions, and where

[133]

it would hand down its decision that day. The attendant standing at the Court door greeted me with a smile. He said:

"Mr. President, I will get you a seat. Where would you prefer it to be?"

"I am not here as the President," I answered. "I am a member of the Bar of this Court."

"Well, there are seats there," he said, and, turning he escorted me to a seat within a few feet of the nine Justices.

When I had been seated for some five or ten minutes, the members of the Court marched in in their usual single-file column and took their respective seats behind the bar. Soon the Chief Justice was reading the decision in the case brought by the State of ——————— against the Government of the United States. I was some time catching a note from the decision to show what the ruling of the Court would be, but finally the Chief Justice read:

> Just how the Congress of the United States would protect this nation from calamity in the event it were restrained from levying such taxes or how the country could have started; just how armies could be raised and supported in time of war and the general welfare promoted in times of peace, if the hands of the

law makers were so restrained....

I needed to hear no more. The common-sense grasp of the Court was apparent from the decision. The Chief Justice wound up his summation of the case with the remark:

> This Court finds the laws in question to be valid and constitutional. The case of the State of ————————— is therefore dismissed at its costs.

As I left the courtroom I passed the clerk's desk and bowed to the members of the Court. It was the shrine to which I had looked with reverence during my days after I began the study of law. The Chief Justice spoke to me:

"Mr. President, the Court is glad to note that you have kept alive your membership at this bar."

"Thank you," I responded. "It's the only institution in which my membership has never been under attack."

MR. PRESIDENT THE COURT IS GLAD YOU ARE A
MEMBER OF THIS BAR."

VII

Wherein We Inspect the Revived and Greater America

The new President prevents boom and s p e c u l a t i o n orgies; he visits the new America; hears from the grateful people.

FOR some several weeks I acted in a capacity of mentor and umpire of the various agencies and departments which moved into action for sustaining America and the lives and comforts of Americans.

Business had remained somewhat stationary for only a few days, when suddenly such a boom of trading on the exchanges began to break out as had not been seen in any normal time. I immediately called in the heads of the banking system, the Chairman of the Securities Commission and the Secretary of the Treasury.

"We must not permit a boom," I said. "Things must be kept slowed to order and sanity. Move into every line and see what is necessary to have only rational revival of our country."

They soon made themselves effective in curbing hasty and unexplained spurts which, in days past, grew into insane speculation.

From every newspaper and magazine came news and diagrams showing the use of more modern machinery and of plans for greater production but with more leisure and shorter hours of labor rather than unemployment.

Demands for machinery and for automobiles and tractors had risen so much as to tax the output of many factories. Mine owners reported that there was such demand for their products that they could not reduce the hours of labor below 40 hours per week even with every labor-saving device they could install.

An adjustment had to be made of labor to be used in several instances. It was a race for inventive blessings to be installed quickly enough to meet a developing labor shortage under the curtailed hours of work and the increase in demands for all things.

But matters were orderly. The public was sure its problems had been solved. Practically no such things as homeless, hungry or unemployed people were mentioned. Their permanent status in many cases awaited certain general adjustment, but so much temporary activity was abroad that none was without comfort or employment.

School and college expansion was proceeding like magic. Adult education was becoming a large institution. The shortened day gave time for the leisure when men in their forties and over returned to learn what was not taught in their teens.

Foreign countries began to send emissaries and statisticians in groups to explore and study the revived America. I had trouble in finding time to see all these friends from other shores and climes. My general answer became:

[140]

"For all I have not told you, the whole explanation is in the Bible."

On a week end I engaged a special train to tour the principal routes of America. My trip would require two weeks. I made no announcement until it was otherwise discovered I was to look over the country. It was my first extended trip from Washington since my inauguration.

We had been out of Washington less than two hours when cheering began alongside the railroad tracks. In villages and towns the railroad platforms were crowded to capacity. I ordered that we should stop everywhere.

At the first stop I said to my secretary:

"I'm going to find out something for myself. Are we really moving the way the people want? I will soon know."

I stepped to the rear of my train and shouted:

"All right, folks, what's wrong?"

Everyone seemed to cheer at once. I shouted again:

"Tell me, what can I do for anyone? What's wrong?"

There was more cheering until a loud voice roared:

"Nothing! We have just found out how bad we needed you for President all the time."

APPENDIX

Wherein a Digest of the Share Our Wealth Legislation is Contained.

LIMITATIONS ON FORTUNES
(Minimum and Maximum)
Redistribution of Wealth

Congress provided that as a matter of national policy necessary for the preservation of the nation and its defense against foreign foes that the United States declare it against public policy for any family to have less than the comforts of home and of life, free of debt, and equal to at least the value of one-third the average American family wealth; that in order to guarantee such comforts and necessities of life to all the people, it was necessary that some reasonable limit be placed on the wealth which one person might own; and, accordingly, Congress declared that it was against the public policy of the United States for any one person to possess wealth in excess of one hundred times the average family fortune.

To bring about the redistribution of wealth, not only to give the comforts of home to the people, but to provide some of the revenue needed for expansion and improvement in the United States, Congress imposed a capital levy tax to be levied every year on every fortune in the nation as follows:

(a) On all wealth owned by a person from 1¢ up to One Million Dollars, no capital tax levy, it being the policy of the law that for one to own up to a million dollars does no injury to the balance of the people having comforts of life.

(b) On all wealth which one owns above One Million Dollars and up to Two Million Dollars, a capital levy tax of 1% on the second million only.

(c) On all wealth which one owns above Two Million Dollars and up to Three Million Dollars, a capital levy tax of 2% on the third million.

(d) On all wealth which one owns above Three Million Dollars and up to Four Million Dollars, a tax of 4% on the fourth million.

(e) On all wealth which one owns above Four Million Dollars and up to Five Million Dollars, a tax of 8% on the fifth million.

(f) On all wealth which one owns above Five Million Dollars and up to Six Million Dollars, a tax of 16% on the sixth million.

(g) On all wealth which one owns above Six Million Dollars and up to Seven Million Dollars, a tax of 32% on the Seventh Million.

(h) On all wealth which one owns above Seven Million Dollars and up to Eight Million Dollars, a tax of 64% on the eighth million.

(i) On all wealth which one owns above Eight Million Dollars, a tax of 99%.

Calculated by simple arithmetic the foregoing table meant that all fortunes would generally fall to a maximum limit of around Five Million Dollars to the person the first or second year, but gradually thereafter, the capital tax, being levied year after year, would reduce the largest fortune to from one to two millions of dollars.

Inasmuch as large quantities of properties could not be converted into cash to make an immediate payment, the person taxed was permitted to turn over property or cash in payment of the tax and was also allowed to pay the tax in installments.

The money and wealth thus raised for the government, under the surveys and plans arranged, was used first to supply the comforts of home and life to the masses up to a value equal to one-third of the average family wealth. The Congress provided that, in order to make such distribution of the properties turned into the United States in payment of the capital levy tax, that the Government should have the right to sell property, to transfer and exchange it for other property, to issue currency to be retired from sale and disposition of the government's properties, along the lines as followed in the Federal Land Bank financing.

It being determined that each family should have a home and comforts for life, the acts of Congress provided that such a home should not be sold by the owners unless the State should consent to such sale, and that the proceeds from such sale should be impounded, only to be used for the purchase of another homestead. The rules set up to protect the ownership of homes and comforts for life in several States were largely followed in preparing this legislation.